The social worker

C R. 1883-1967 Attlee

THE SOCIAL SERVICE LIBRARY

I. THE SOCIAL WORKER

THE SOCIAL SERVICE LIBRARY

Edited by
C. R. ATTLEE, M.A.

FIRST FIVE VOLUMES.

1. **THE SOCIAL WORKER.**
   By C. R. Attlee.

2. **THE BOY.**
   By Rev. R. R. Hyde.

3. **THE MOTHER AND THE INFANT.**
   By Miss E. V. Eckhard.

4. **THE GIRL.**
   By Miss C. K. Dewar.

5. **THE WORKER AND THE STATE.**
   By Prof. Frank Tillyard.

Published in conjunction with
THE RATAN TATA DEPT. OF SOCIAL SCIENCE,
UNIVERSITY OF LONDON.

THE SOCIAL WORKER

BY

C. R. ATTLEE, M.A.

LONDON
G. BELL AND SONS, LTD.
1920

PREFACE

THIS book, which is the first of a series dealing with social questions, is intended to be not only a general introduction to the subject of social service but to deal more particularly with the social worker. It aims at providing those who are contemplating participation in social work of some kind with a general sketch of the opportunities of service that present themselves. These will be dealt with in more detail in subsequent volumes. It is also an attempt to show what are the qualifications and training desirable in the social worker.

Although this series is issued under the aegis of the University of London Ratan Tata Department of Social Science and Administration, the opinions expressed in each volume are those of the authors, and must not be taken as committing the Department generally to them. In my opinion, for a book on a social subject to have any value it must necessarily express the personal views and experience of the writer, and, despite his endeavours to be impartial, the author may very possibly appear biassed to those who do not share his outlook.

C. R. ATTLEE.

CONTENTS

CHAPTER V

THE QUALIFICATIONS AND TRAINING OF THE SOCIAL WORKER

CHAPTER VI

RELIGIOUS AGENCIES

CHAPTER VII

THE SETTLEMENT MOVEMENT

CHAPTER VIII

VARIETIES OF SOCIAL WORKERS

CHAPTER IX

THE SOCIAL SERVICE OF THE WORKING CLASSES

CHAPTER I

SOCIAL SERVICE AND CITIZENSHIP

THE term social service that forms part of the title of this series requires some examination. In its simplest meaning it comprises every contribution that each member of a society, individually or working through a group, brings to society—in so far as his or her work is not an absolute disservice. The miner who wins coal from the pit, the farmer who grows food, the railwayman who assists in its transportation, and the business man who facilitates the exchange and distribution of commodities, are all engaged in social service as much as the civil servant, the member of a governing body or the charitable worker; but in actual every-day speech the term has been narrowed down to denote a fairly distinct sphere of human activity. If one hears of anyone engaged in social work, a very definite picture is formed in the mind; one sees the man who gives up his evenings to the work of a boy's club, or the woman engaged in district visiting or assisting at a school clinic or infant welfare centre. The term suggests the secretary of a Charity Organisation committee, the hospital almoner, or the probation officer. Social service presents itself as either an occupation for the leisure of the better-fed classes, or a specialised employment for certain professionals. Particularly it suggests persons of a superior position in society engaged in the endeavour to ameliorate the lot of the poor.

The picture may not be thought very inviting, rather drab, dusty and uninspiring, with a touch of the patronising and unco' guid about it. In the foreground of the picture are a number of people in sad-coloured garments with a parson or two among them sitting round a deal table in an aroma of soap and water or disinfectant, obviously engaged in doing their duty towards their neighbours, who are represented in the background by a shabby and ill-at-ease group of mothers and children, with an infrequent and deplorably humble man.

"Social workers," someone will say rather pityingly, "good people no doubt in their way, but very dull, forever fussing over their lame ducks; all very well, of course, for people who like that sort of thing, elderly spinsters and men with no settled occupation." This or something like it is a not uncommon view, but it is, I believe, a profound misconception. The Social Service movement of modern times is not confined to any one class, nor is it the preserve of a particular section of dull and respectable people. It has arisen out of a deep discontent with society as at present constituted, and among its prophets have been the greatest spirits of our time. It is not a movement concerned alone with the material, with housing and drains, clinics and feeding centres, gas and water, but is the expression of the desire for social justice, for freedom and beauty, and for the better apportionment of all the things that make up a good life. It is the constructive side of the criticism passed by the reformer and the revolutionary on the failure of our industrialised society to provide a fit environment where a good life shall be possible for all.

Poetry has been called a criticism of life, and in the work of the great poets of the nineteenth century we can see the discontent caused by this failure getting stronger and stronger as the fruits of modern industrialism began to ripen. The note is struck in the earliest of the new school that renewed the poetry of imagination after the long sleep of Georgian artificiality. William Blake, visionary and prophet, declared :

> I will not cease from mental fight,
> Nor shall the sword sleep in my hand,
> Till we have built Jerusalem,
> In England's green and pleasant land.

In the poetry of Keats may be observed the gradual invasion of misgivings as to the rightness of the position of the dreamer, striving to create beauty, but turning his back on the parallel creation of ugliness, moral and material.

Thus in " Isabella and the Pot of Basil " the summary of the murderous brothers' worldly position is startlingly modern, and is capable of, and clearly intended to bear, a wider application :

> With her two brothers this fair lady dwelt,
> Enrichéd from ancestral merchandise,
> And for them many a weary hand did swelt
> In torchéd mines and noisy factories—
>
> For them alone did seethe
> A thousand men in troubles wide and dark,
> Half-ignorant, they turned an easy wheel,
> That set sharp racks at work, to pinch and peel.

While in "The Fall of Hyperion" the note becomes even clearer.

> "Are there not thousands in the world," said I,
> "Who love their fellows even to the death,
> Who feel the giant agony of the world,
> And more, like slaves to poor humanity,
> Labour for mortal good?"

In Shelley an even more militant note is sounded, in such poems as "Men of England, wherefore plough," or "The Masque of Anarchy," or "Queen Mab." Here we have the spirit of revolt against social injustice, not intruding on the poet's vision, as in Keats, but animating and inspiring all his work. Later comes a still more striking figure, the greatest of the modern prophets, Ruskin. A man extremely sensitive to beauty, greatly gifted in its portrayal, is torn from his contemplation of the scenery, the architecture and the paintings that he loves by a horror of the ugliness around him, a disgust at the injustice of the social system under which he lives, and feels an imperious need to do all that he can to denounce the evil and sweep it away. As he says himself, "I feel the force of machinery and the fury of avaricious commerce to be so irresistible that I have seceded from the study, not only of architecture but of art, as I would in a besieged city, to seek the best mode of getting bread and butter for the multitude." Thus he was led to denounce the current economic theory, and in "Unto this last" shook its ascendancy, while he demonstrated in "The Stones of Venice" and the "Seven Lamps of Architecture" that the root of ugliness was social injustice, and that beauty depended on freedom and justice. But further, in contrast to the mere rebels who only denounced, he definitely attempted to put his ideals into practice. His co-operative commonwealth failed and cost him a fortune, but it is just this determination to make practical experiment as well as to theorise, to do as well as to think, that is the kernel of social service. William Morris, again, was drawn from the practice of the many arts in which he delighted, and of which he was master, to the uncongenial duty of street-corner agitation, for which he was little fitted.

Now, in all these cases it will be observed that it is precisely the finest, most sensitive and most daring spirits of their age who feel the call for change. The social worker is in high company, and social service is not the preserve of the parish worker, the charity-monger and the statistician, but is the legacy of the prophets. Social service is not the monopoly of the few, nor is it confined to any one class; it is not a particular set of activities so much as an attitude of mind to all human actions. It is the demand that their existence as members of society, and as members of a particular part of that society, makes on all men and women. It is essentially the duty of citizenship not only to the city and the State but to the world.

In the course of this book we shall be obliged to use the term "social worker" in its narrow sense, but it is necessary to emphasise at the outset that although this may be done, the more extended meaning will be kept in view.

The development of the social service idea from the old position of the charitable worker must now be considered, and we will turn to the examination of some of the factors that have altered the outlook of the social worker from the time when his principal object was benevolence down to the modern conception of social justice.

THE CHARITY IDEA

Before the industrial revolution the goodwill of the ordinary man and woman that is the main factor in social service, expressed itself in acts of charity. For each particular need that arose our forefathers devised some form of voluntary organisation or relied on the efforts of charitable individuals.

Thus, when it was observed that there were a number of uncared-for, and unwanted infants the Foundling Hospital was started: for the needs of the sick, hospitals and provident dispensaries were set up, and for the aged almshouses were built, while unusual distress would be met by the free issue of soup, or by gifts of clothing or blankets. In a comparatively static society this method of individual provision worked fairly well; although there were many poor there was not very much destitution, and for the destitute provision had been made by the poor law of Queen Elizabeth's reign. In general the kindness of neighbours and the benevolence of the well-to-do were sufficient to deal with the normal cases of distress, and provide relief according to the not very extended conception of necessary comfort that obtained. When, however, the whole structure of society was altered by the agrarian revolution that broke up the old life of the countryside, and the industrial revolution which collected huge numbers of people together into particular districts, and divided society rigidly into two main classes, a small landlord and employing class, and a proletariat, the system that was suitable for small, almost self-contained communities was powerless to grapple with the host of new problems raised by a complicated system of industry and the emergence of the Great Society. While industry was on a small scale masters and men were intimately acquainted with each other, and there was little need of intervention from outside; there was no place for factory inspection, and little possibility of combined action on the part of the workers. In a small society custom and public opinion are enough to regulate the relationships between man and man in the ordinary affairs of life in accordance with elementary ideas of justice. Here and there, it is true, the powerful and unscrupulous person may dominate a small community, and work his will; but it is far harder than in large societies where the details are so many and the system so complicated that few people see much outside the narrow round of their own preoccupations.

At the beginning of the nineteenth century the conception of society as divided into classes, each with its own particular function, held sway, and charity was regarded as an act of grace on the part of the rich to their poorer neighbours. The tide of opinion was running strongly in favour of *laisser faire*, old regulations as to wages and hours of labour, formerly fixed by the justices of the peace, were being swept away, old restrictions on industry were found to be obsolete, owing to the changes in the methods of production, and the geographical distribution of industries, and the country was committed more and more to the forces of unrestrained competition. The optimistic doctrine that if each individual sought his own good the interests of the community as a whole would be best served was generally accepted, and the only mitigation to the harshness of economic law admitted was the charity of individuals.

If we examine in a little more detail the charitable idea we shall see how essentially it belongs to a certain conception of society. The charitable motive is primarily religious. Christianity lays down that charity in its widest sense is necessary to salvation, and that almsgiving is one of the duties of the Christian, so that throughout the ages of faith one finds a large amount of charitable work done with the principal object of benefiting the soul of the giver, the effect on the welfare of the recipient being a secondary consideration. Christianity shares this conception of charity with other oriental religions, and in so far as the object is the good of the benefactor rather than that of the beneficiary it is very far from the social service idea, although its effects may, or more probably may not be, socially desirable. Thus the frequent English charitable donation by will of a sum of money to be laid out in loaves or bread for the poor, sometimes coupled with the obligation to pray for the soul of the testator, must be classed with the casual pence bestowed upon the beggar by someone who can well spare it. In both cases the element of self-sacrifice which is implicit in social service is absent, indeed, this is absent in all charitable gifts that are given out of superfluity of riches, or out of wealth which the donor cannot take away with him, so that the only people to be denied anything are the residuary legatees. Akin to these are the numerous benefactions which are given in order to quiet the mind from uneasiness at the sight of wretchedness, or to satisfy a queasy conscience that, recognising that all is not well, endeavours to obtain a cheap insurance against disturbing thoughts, or a mild glow of satisfaction at the feeling that some good has been done, and that gratitude has been merited. As an early Victorian children's book puts it, "For Mary truly understood the luxury of doing good."

There is a great difference between this sort of charity and that of those who actually take the trouble to find out what is amiss before trying to devise appropriate remedies, and who themselves perform their own almsgiving.

Charity at its highest is the expression of the love for one's fellows that is at the root of all vital social work; but, at the period with which we are dealing, it had become narrowed down in most cases to mere almsgiving. The old incentive to charity that we find in the mediaeval church became weaker when at the Reformation the doctrine of salvation by faith caused less stress to be laid on works, and although at the latter end of the eighteenth century it was reinforced by the philanthropic impulse which was so powerful a motive with men like Jonas Hanway and Romilly, the general view of charity was not a high one.

Society as constituted was accepted, and the existence of the poor taken for granted, nay even welcomed as providing an outlet for the benevolence of the rich. Charity is always apt to be accompanied by a certain complacence and condescension on the part of the benefactor, and by an expectation of gratitude from the recipient which cuts at the root of all true friendliness. The charitable of the time seem to us to-day to be smug and self-satisfied. They delighted in sermons to the poor on convenient virtues, and lacked that sharp self-criticism that is the note of society to-day. The change from this attitude to social service has been effected not only by the utter failure of charity to cope with the difficult problems of poverty (a failure that does not mean the condemnation of the charitable, for it was inherent in the very nature of the problem), but also by an entirely changed outlook, due to three principal causes—the work of the social reformers, the advances in knowledge, and the rise of democratic ideas.

SOCIAL REFORM MOVEMENTS

The change from the charity conception mentioned above to that of social service has been effected particularly by the work of the social reformers. Our attitude to social service will be different according to the conception that we have of society. If we regard it as at present constituted as on the whole just and right, and approve of the present economic structure, social work will seem to us, as it were, a work of supererogation, a praiseworthy attempt to ease the minor injustices inevitable in all systems of society. We shall see a series of more or less disconnected problems not related to any one general question. On the other hand, we may see as the root of the trouble an entirely wrong system altogether, a mistaken aim, a faulty standard of values, and we shall form in our minds more or less clearly a picture of some different system, a society organised on a new basis altogether, guided by other incentives than those that operate at the present time, and we shall relate all our particular efforts to this point of view.

All social reformers belong to one or other of these schools of thought ; the dividing line may be a narrow one in some cases, but is sufficiently visible. The movements for reform of the earlier half of the nineteenth century were carried on mainly by those who held the first view, who dealt with particular social evils but did not attack the basis of society as a whole. Thus the prison reformers, Howard and Mrs. Fry, the factory reformers, Shaftesbury, Oastler and Sadler, all belong to the first class. Shaftesbury was able to carry out his work of agitation for the enforcement of decent conditions in the factories and mines without consciously working for State intervention in industrial matters, and indeed without the realisation that he was sapping the foundations of the *laisser faire* attitude of the State, and starting the building of the great edifice of regulation and inspection which has extended over almost every part of the national life. On the other hand, Robert Owen, who laid the foundations of so many fruitful movements for the bettering of conditions in factories, of education and co-operative distribution and production, was able to relate all his activities to his " New View of Society," and was essentially revolutionist in his attitude.

As the century proceeds a vast amount of practical reform in every field of activity was brought about through the disconnected efforts of little groups of reformers, most of them intent on the abolition of some particular abuse or the introduction of some advance in social organisation. Some grappled with the evil of pauperism and endeavoured to organise the goodwill of the ordinary man and woman so as to make charity effective, others attacked the evils of the housing conditions in the towns. Others, like Dr.

Barnardo, were affected by the sight of some particular evil (as in his case of children sleeping out in the streets), and devoted their whole lives to a particular piece of social work.

As the time goes on we can see a steady tendency at work for social reformers to feel the need of collective rather than individual action. The man or woman who is interested in one particular piece of reform inevitably comes in contact with others who are working in the same field, but with different methods and a different point of view: he begins to realise what a small part of the evil he is able to affect by his work, and is driven to recognise that it is only by the co-operation of individuals with the community generally that the special reforms which he has at heart can be brought about. He discovers that instead of a particular evil being, as he thought, peculiar to his own district, it is only a part of a wider problem, which as an individual he is powerless to solve, so that he finds himself obliged to turn to the organised community to help him. Thus to-day the social reformer is less apt to rely on his own individual efforts than to endeavour to arouse the nation to act by passing laws to prevent the occurrence of certain abuses or to empower local authorities to take action.

Again, the individual citizen or the social reform society may set to work to prove the practicability of certain reforms, and may then wish to see them adopted generally; but it is found that precisely where such a reform is most needed it is impossible to get it put into action, owing to the indifference or even hostility of a particular class or locality. The need of some form of compulsion is felt. A good instance is that of the notification of births, which was first pioneered by individuals, then made permissive so that the districts that were enthusiastic for child welfare could adopt it, and finally made mandatory to force the indifferent to take action. Thus while there is still much work done by voluntary individual enthusiasts, the whole tendency of late has been to translate the ideas of social reformers into legislative and administrative action.

The social reformers of the present day have little fear of State interference, and generally speaking are far more ready than in the past to face big changes. Robert Owen and his fellow-workers in their day, the Christian Socialists in the 50's were voices crying in the wilderness. To-day the ideas that prompted their reforming efforts are more and more widely accepted. Most social reformers are ready to accept a very large amount of control by the community over the activities of the individual, and to recognise the need for a greater recognition of the rights and duties of all citizens. The question to-day is thus rather one of the method and proportion than of complete denial and assertion. Society is far more self-conscious than it was in the past, and the social conscience is at work among men and women of all classes. The Settlement movement was an early expression of this, and the increased searchings of heart in the Churches as to the relationship between the principles of Christianity and business, and the difficulty of reconciling the two, are becoming more and more evident. The demand of the social reformer to-day is for a new attitude to social problems rather than for specific reforms in any particular department of life.

ADVANCES IN KNOWLEDGE

Looking back on the conditions of the early part of last century and reading of the years of effort that it took to prevent small children, even under seven years of age, from being worked for fourteen or fifteen hours a day in factories and mines, we are amazed at the callousness with which such a state of affairs was regarded, and can hardly conceive how people who were, as we can see, in other affairs intelligent, reasonably humane and enlightened, should not have instantly protested. Yet at the same time we are ourselves indifferent to numbers of evils to which we have become accustomed, and which are rarely noticed. Probably in a future time it will seem amazing to our descendants that we should have allowed huge slum-areas like East and South London, the Lancashire towns, or the mining villages, to remain for years without taking real action to abolish them. We all imagine that if we had been present in Jerusalem we should not have voted for Barabbas.

In our criticisms of the social workers of the past we are apt to forget how great has been the increase in knowledge since their day. The careful dissection and investigation of social phenomena is a comparatively modern achievement, but it has perhaps done more than any single factor to change the outlook of men and women on social problems. Early reformers were working in the dark, grappling with evils that had come on society with great suddenness. The causes underlying social discontents had not been investigated, and even the facts were not known to more than a few.

To-day the social worker can profit by the labours

of his predecessor, the ground has been explored and mapped out. Research has been made into almost every phase of poverty, and many of its causes have been elucidated.

The older type of social worker was mainly endeavouring to deal with results: he saw that people were hungry, or ill-clad, or sick, and his first impulse was to provide food, clothing and medicine. The existence of classes of the community habitually in this state was taken for granted, and the reasons why they were so were not investigated. The result too often was that the remedy, dealing as it did with symptoms only, was as bad as the disease. In the same way, many social reformers did not sufficiently realise that the evil which appeared to them to be a cause was in itself only a result. Thus the prevalence of drunkenness would be asserted as a prime cause of poverty, without considering whether in fact drunkenness itself was not due to bad conditions of work, a degrading environment, or the general greyness of life.

During the nineteenth century a great advance was made in the science of preventive medicine. Instead of being concerned almost entirely with healing disease after it had arisen, medical science turned to the improvement of the environment, and the prevention of disease arising. Thus the recognition that a whole group of diseases were bred in the slums, and were due to a low standard of life, led to the public health agitation, and the passing of legislation promoting sanitary reform which has done far more to improve the health of the urban population than any great advances in curative methods. By anology from this in social matters we can see that unemployment, for instance, is a disease of an industrial society in our present stage of development, and that no amount of provision for individual men and women will take the place of the removal as far as possible of its causes. In the words of Mr. Sidney Webb it is no good hammering on the bulge, the direct method is often the ineffective one. There are numbers of social workers who find in the work of research and investigation the best outlet for their desire for social service. Some may be chiefly engaged in investigation into the psychological effects of certain pieces of social machinery, others in the machinery itself. It is almost a distinct motive in itself, this desire to see the machinery of society running smoothly and cleanly.

Such a feeling can be seen running through the works of Mr. H. G. Wells, where he exhibits the disgust of an orderly and scientific mind at the wasteful and chaotic nature of our social arrangements. One has only to compare his Utopias with that of William Morris to see the difference between the scientific and aesthetic appeals to social service. In those of the former the emphasis is on the mechanism of society, and the possibilities of harnessing the forces of nature in order to make attainable a fine life for human beings are worked out in considerable detail and with great imagination. In Morris, on the other hand, there is little attention to the machinery of society, but a very keen realisation of the sort of life he thought best for people. Thus the scientific motive takes its place as one of the incentives that lead men to devote themselves to social service, and the great influence of the scientific investigator on the methods of social reformers, and on the outlook of those engaged in social work, must be acknowledged.

It has been pointed out above how much the doctrines of the classical economists hampered the efforts of social reformers by practically forbidding all action by the State outside the narrowest lines. Economics became known as the dismal science: it was thought to be opposed to the efforts of the more earnest reformers, and to render futile all the endeavours of the working classes to improve their industrial position: hence the vehement attacks on it by Ruskin and others. At one time it seemed as if economic science had got entirely out of touch with human life: it had become abstract and academic. To the man who keenly realised the evils of the industrial system the doctrines of the classical economists seemed to offer little hope of better things. He read for instance of the fluidity of labour, and that if labour was displaced from one industry it would flow to wherever it was needed; that if new processes and increased machinery were introduced, in the long run more men would be employed; but to the man in touch with the sufferings of the unemployed this was cold comfort, for he knew that the long run was often fatal to the man with the short purse. The economist did not seem to realise that the abstract concept of labour consisted of a number of human beings who were in fact the greater part of the nation. Political economy seemed to be inhuman, in laying stress on how commodities could be most cheaply produced, without enquiring what would be the effect on social conditions.

From this position the science has been rescued through the work of the practical social worker, the experimenter, and the investigator. The transition from the earlier to the later views of J. S. Mill marks the turning of the tide, and since that time the science has become more and more social. It has become the hopeful science.

This changed outlook has been reflected in the policy of the country in regard to social questions. From complete freedom of contract we have moved to an ever increasing state regulation of conditions. The earlier efforts at regulation of hours of labour, wages, and conditions of work were regarded at the time as rather regrettable exceptional provisions, introduced for the protection of certain classes who were especially weak, women and children. To-day the idea of a minimum wage and a maximum working day is almost generally accepted. In the same way during the last thirty years the work of the organised community in local affairs has steadily increased, and the question whether a certain industry should be carried on by individual enterprise or collective effort is decided more on grounds of practical convenience than general principle. Where formerly it was considered that the State was a sort of referee who kept the ring wherein contending individualities had full scope for contest, we now have the conception that it is the duty of the State to act as the co-ordinating factor in making all individual efforts work for the good of the citizens.

This idea of a conscious endeavour to promote by governmental action the production of the best possible environment for the breeding of good citizens was shortly expressed by the present Prime Minister when he said that we could not produce an A1 nation from C3 conditions. It may be claimed that this does not amount to a great change of outlook, that all states have this aim to promote the best life for the citizens, but the point that differentiates a statement like this from the speeches of the statesmen of sixty years ago, is that to-day we consider that it is possible for the community by collective action to alter men's environment, whereas then it was thought that any interference with environment would be acting against nature, and against all sound economic principles.

THE PROGRESS OF DEMOCRACY

The rise of democracy has changed the outlook of the social worker: formerly social work was done *for* now *with* the working classes. This is due to several factors. First to the efforts of the workers themselves; during the last hundred years the working classes have gradually built up their own organs of collective expression, their own machinery of government, and have, to some extent, evolved their own philosophy of society. The poor are not now an inert mass on which the kindly disposed may exert moral or material pressure, or mould to their own liking. Through their associations, trade co-operative and political, they have trained their own leaders, and express their own views as to the general and particular policy of the community.

The social worker of to-day has to recognise that among the working classes are men and women as well equipped as himself, and as awake to the problems of the day. From parliament down to the parish council working men and women are engaged in the actual work of legislation and administration; in industry they are claiming a large share in the control over their own lives and over the governance of industry, and in education they are claimihg an equality of opportunity. It is unnecessary to labour this point, it has been driven home recently by numberless instances, the most significant of all, perhaps, being that the British delegates at the peace treaty of Versailles included a working man. We have only to cast back in our minds to the treaty of Vienna to realise what this means. In a word, to-day working men and women claim full citizenship. They are not content to be legislated for by special acts of Parliament designed to protect them, far less to be mere recipients of charity. They refuse to be regarded as a special class with special functions.

The second factor is the narrowing of the gulf of ignorance that formerly was so deep between classes. In a recent investigation in Sheffield of the habits and mentality of some particular streets it was found that twenty-five per cent. belonged to Class I, which comprised the well equipped who were informed on questions of the day, read a good deal, were fairly educated, in a word were qualified citizens. It is doubtful whether other classes put to the same test would yield much better results. The small minority in each class that reads and thinks has access to the same books and understands a common language: members from the well-to-do classes can find working men who will be prepared to discuss problems of economics, philosophy, or natural science in an intelligent way, just as others in each class would find a common ground in the works of the late Nat Gould or in the pages of the "Pink 'Un."

A third factor is the greatly increased travelling facilities, which have not only brought people from different parts of the country together, but has helped to mingle classes.

Thus in the growth of the social service idea the working-class attitude has its place and has contributed valuable ideas.

CITIZENSHIP

The fact that we live in societies implies that we have certain rights and duties as members. I do not intend here to go into the old controversy as to natural, political, and legal rights, or to discuss the theory of the social contract. The object of our coming together and living in a society is that we may have a better chance of obtaining the means to live a good life than if we remain isolated. We claim the right to as full an opportunity of expressing our personalities as has anybody else, and that implies the duty of securing as good an opportunity for others as we have ourselves. Society is built up on a series of rights and duties express or implied; they may vary at different stages of human development and between different classes, but at our present stage of development in which all do at least lip-service to democracy, our ideal is the fullest opportunity for the development of every human soul. It is possible to have societies based on a different principle organised for the benefit of a single class, for the use of which the remainder are subordinated. In one society the subordinate class may be slaves, in another nominally free but really subject, in yet another the women may be considered as unworthy of the rights of citizenship and only existing for the pleasure of men. But in our present stage the rights and duties of citizenship are conceived of as belonging to and incumbent upon all.

But although we may all admit the object of society and the duties of citizenship the content of that duty is very variously interpreted. Some people will emphasise one duty, some another. One aspect of the duty of the citizen has been very much emphasised of late, that of the defence of the political community against attack by armed forces. During the late war it was accepted by everybody that private interests must be subordinated to the good of the community; it was urged, and by none so loudly as by those whose conception of citizenship had not previously been highly developed, that it was the duty of every man to do his service in the trenches or munition works, and it was recognised that all forms of work in the country must subserve one aim, the success of the nation in war. The able-bodied man or woman who did not in current phrase do his or her bit was looked upon almost in the same light as the profiteer who devoted himself to piling up a big fortune out of his country's extremity. All this appeared perfectly natural to those who made the appeal and those who responded to it, yet few had any definite theory of the relation of the citizen to the State, so much so that those who claimed allegiance to a duty that they considered overrode even their duty as citizens of England failed to make people understand their position. The idea that it was the duty of the individual to give not merely his service but his life for the benefit of the rest of the community or even for the benefit of humanity did not seem strange at the time. What was strange was that this was a new attitude, something temporary adopted for an emergency, even something unnatural.

It appeared to most people before the war and

apparently to many since—perfectly natural, right and reasonable that the interest of the individual should come first, that of the community second, that in normal times citizenship should be passive, an affair of votes now and again, that the service of society should be so unimportant that it should merely take up the fag-end of a man's time, or to be so exceptional a vacation that those who endeavoured to give their services should be regarded as a special class, the social workers.

It appeared natural to most people that the ordinary citizen should pursue his own interests without regard to their effect on society, that the prevailing motive should be self interest, and that the idea of regarding one's ordinary work as an act of social service was confined to very few.

As Professor Urwick points out :

" In our modern national life the sense of unity is not realised, and the all pervading duties of citizenship are lost sight of in the wilderness of interests of both individuals and groups. Our extraordinarily complex life, our far too numerous activities, our strong assertion of individual liberty which we very imperfectly understand, and the assumed importance of our occupation as self-seekers and self-developers—all these things tend to drive the citizen idea into the background. Yet in theory and also in fact it is still the necessary and single basis of social duty and social morality. Perhaps also the looseness of most social ties and bonds, the plasticity and vagueness of most communal relationships, make it additionally hard for us to think of the great duties, and easier to think of duties as those of the smaller, inner circles, such as the family or the workshop. And so nowadays we have to search for the citizen-duties underneath or behind those others, just as we have to go out and search for our neighbours to whom Samaritan kindnesses are due."[1]

This attitude of mind, this habit of regarding society as something with which the individual citizen was not concerned, can be traced in part at least to the dominant idea of the nineteenth century, the exaltation of the individual at the expense of society, and the theory that the less the organised community interfered with the individual the better. The prevailing theory that the industrial welfare of the country could best be served by each individual pursuing his own interests led to a weakening of the conception of citizenship. It was assumed that progress came about through the unconscious action of individuals rather than through the active endeavours of groups. This emphasis on individual action and deprecation of interference by the State led to a conception of social service as something extra, a work of supererogation, and a line was drawn between the narrow field in which collective action could function and the wider field for initiative of the charitable and philanthropic. Charitable work being looked upon as a virtue not as a duty, took away from the dignity of citizenship.

To-day we have travelled far from those ideas, the awakening of the social conscience so conspicuous in the later days of the nineteenth century, and turned more and more to community action. The confident belief that our progress is necessarily in the right direction, that evolution inevitably moves towards a higher and better state, is less assured. The note of

[1] *Philosophy of Social Progress*, E. J. Urwick. Methuen.

confidence has become weaker and weaker as investigation has revealed the other side of the enormous industrial development of modern times. The motive of self-interest has been shown to work in a very partial manner, now for good and now for evil, and a search is being made for something to replace it. The problem of motive is the great one to-day. Over the greater part of the field of industry the motive of self-interest does not operate. To the entrepreneur it is still sufficient to produce the necessary energy though it does nothing to ensure that this energy will be well directed. To the wage-earners who are the great majority of the citizens of the modern State profit making, if not impossible, is unattractive; their energies were stimulated formerly far more by fear of losing their places in industry and falling into the ranks of the unemployed than by any hope of increasing their gains: their increased knowledge of the industrial system and their demand for an increase of leisure and life rather than more work and more pay are symptoms of the new outlook: appeals made for increased output fall on deaf ears, the motive is absent and therefore our industrial machinery is creaking.

The problem of society to-day is not so much material as psychological. We have the means of producing all the material necessities of a good life, food, clothing and houses in abundance; luxuries as much as we please, and the means of enjoyment of art and literature could be open to all. The one thing necessary is the getting of the human will to operate.

Now there is another motive that operates over a considerable field of human activity and that is Service. We are wont to pride ourselves on the number of men who have this instinct for service, rich men who undertake the burdens of State when they might live on their estates, the men who undertake the less burdensome but more tedious duties of local justice and administration. We call the military and naval establishments services, and boast of the traditions of devotion to duty and sacrifice for the common weal of our civil service at home and abroad. That this motive exists is admitted, and this is the motive that makes for good citizenship and social service in the narrow sense is one of its manifestations.

It is then to the spirit of social service, in my opinion, that we must look for the new motive to replace, or at least reinforce, that of self-interest. We have demands made by bodies of workers that their industries should be turned into public services. During the war the makers of munitions were stimulated to greater exertions and submitted to long hours and intense work by appeals to their desire to do service to their country and their comrades in the field, while many a man who fought and died in the war did so in the main because he believed he was serving the cause of humanity.

It is true that in all these cases other motives are at work, self-interest, the desire for distinction, the lesser loyalties, but in a greater or less degree the spirit of social service is present.

Thus the more we can get the idea of social service as the main motive for all our work, the more likely are we to find a peaceable solution to our present discontents. We have to realise that we cannot divide up the various spheres of human work into water-tight compartments, some carried on solely for the benefit of the individual, others solely for the good of the community; both motives must be present the maker of machinery or boots must regard his work from the standpoint of its satisfying certain wants of the community as well as supplying him with a living, just as the doctor, although he adopts his profession as a means of earning an income, regards it also as a service to humanity, and binds himself to exercise it in a way that shall be most conducive to the well being of all. His professional traditions prevent him from exploiting a new discovery as a monopoly for his own benefit no less than they inhibit him from spreading disease in order to obtain fees for curing it.

In social service, then, we particularly emphasise the position of men and women as citizens. In our society to-day we have many interests, and are joined together in many different circles, social, religious, economic, aesthetic, or civic, so that our good will is apt to be dissipated by this distribution, but in each of these spheres the spirit of social service is present, and constitutes the force by which the group is formed, and through the power of which it operates. But whatever smaller groups we belong to, we are all united as members of the State.

What, then, is the relationship between social service in the broader sense which we have just been considering and social service in the narrow almost professional meaning? Just this; that the social worker is one who feels the claims of society upon him more than others, he brings to all his work this conception of his duty as a member of a civilised society to make his contribution to the well being of his fellows.

At this time there are many men and women who have received a strong impression from the war period, of their duty to work unselfishly for the community, men who have been in the army or navy, women who have been occupied in nursing in the hospitals or have been serving in one or other of the auxiliary services, and others of the older generations who have been doing various forms of war work, are finding a certain blank in their lives now these interests have come to an end. I heard a girl who had grown to womanhood during the war ask after the armistice, " What did people do before the War ? " She did not wish to go in for the more or less futile social life that was the lot of many in pre-war days, and could not conceive of life without work.

The series of books of which this is the introductory volume is an attempt to show what has been done in the past and what is being done now in various fields of social work, to discuss some of the problems that affect different groups of people at certain ages or in certain capacities, and to describe the methods of solution that are being adopted. It is in fact an endeavour to answer the question asked by many people, " What can I do to perform my duty as a citizen ? "

In each volume some particular set of problems will be discussed ; thus in one volume will be found an account of the agencies dealing with the mother and the infant, in another the provision for the sick, while others will deal with the various associations of working-men and women, in order that those who wish to take up social work may find in them material for judging what work will give most scope for their abilities, and most enlist their enthusiasm.

CHAPTER II

CHARITIES

IN this chapter the word 'Charity' will not be used in its abstract sense as denoting a moral quality, but rather in the more popular and concrete meaning of almsgiving, whether the alms given are money, time, or service. It may at first seem difficult to draw any hard and fast distinction between charities and other branches of social service, but the popular acceptance of the word is well understood, and is in practice confined to the work of societies or institutions supported by voluntary contributions and carried on for the purpose of dealing with individuals suffering from some of the various ills to which human beings are subject, whether in mind, body or estate, and for the meeting of these needs by appropriate action. The essence of charities is their voluntary nature. Thus it is a confusion of thought to call the Poor Law or free meals for school children State charity, or the provision of asylums for the feeble-minded municipal charity. In these cases the organised community has made provision for some of the eventualities of life, and has given its citizens the right to avail themselves under certain conditions of these provisions.

In charity there is no right; whatever is provided is a gift. It is true that there are charitable endowments to which certain persons have a right, but this right is private, not public, and secured by the testamentary provision of the donor, not by the act of the State.

Again, social service means personal service, whether the personal service is supplemented by material gifts, or not, whereas charity, in the sense of almsgiving, may mean merely money gifts wherein there is no personal sacrifice of time or thought, but the mere act of giving. In Social Service the labour of thinking out what is to be done, and doing the work, cannot be delegated; in charity it very frequently is.

In a civilised community, although it may be composed of self-reliant individuals, there will be some persons who will be unable at some period of their lives to look after themselves, and the question as to what is to happen to them may be solved in three ways—they may be neglected, they may be cared for by the organised community as of right, or they may be left to the goodwill of individuals in the community. Thus, the sick, the blind, the aged, or the poor may in a primitive society be left to shift for themselves, or may even be left to die or be killed. This may even happen in an advanced society under the influence of ideas of the survival of the fittest. In a purely anarchist society where a high degree of voluntary mutual aid is maintained, all these classes might be left to the care of their fellow anarchists with safety, or in a completely collectivist State provision might be made by the State for the support of the individual under these evil conditions. But in actual fact, in the ordinary state of the modern world we find a mixture of all three methods ; some evils will be neglected altogether, some left to charity, and others dealt with by the State authorities. In England, while there are many evils still neglected, we are in a stage where provision by voluntary effort shows a tendency to pass slowly into recognition of the responsibility of the State for the citizen. But although this tendency is observable it is very far from being complete, and the provision for very many of the unfortunate or the unfit of society is still left to private benevolence, or in some cases to private benevolence in conjunction with the State or municipality. How large is this field of charity can be seen by a glance at the pages of the "Annual Charities Register and Digest," which shows hundreds of societies catering for every sort of unfortunate person. In this country the normal course has been to leave all matters to be dealt with by individuals or voluntary organisations of individuals, and it is not until some evil has proved so great that private charity has failed to cope with it, that the State steps in, either by practically taking over the sporadic and tentative efforts of the charities and giving them form and general application, or by taking steps towards the prevention of the causes of the particular evil that has come to light. It is the common failure of charities to deal with results rather than causes, partly because charity deals mainly with individuals, and draws much of its support from the sentiments of pity evoked by the sight of these people in the hearts of the charitably disposed, and partly because it is only after much investigation of the results that causes emerge, and when they have emerged they are frequently not susceptible of treatment by the voluntary action of individuals.

To give an instance, there is a large number of blind persons in this country and many societies endeavouring to alleviate their condition by the provision of homes, education, or training. Many of them have been blind from birth, and a large proportion of those born blind are so because their parents have been afflicted by venereal disease; but the stamping out of venereal disease is an extremely difficult matter, possible only by a general campaign and by complete measures being taken which are practically impossible to a voluntary organisation. Here the cause does not lie on the surface and has to be left mainly to the State. Again the numerous funds for the unemployed did little good and a great deal of harm, but at the time they were raised the question had not been studied in detail, and the causes, lying deep in our system of industry, had not come to light; the spectacle of the unemployed man made an appeal to the charitable, and it was possible to attempt alleviation, but the prevention of unemployment could not be attempted by voluntary methods, and indeed has only recently been recognised as a possibility by the State itself. Two features will strike the reader of the charities register mentioned above, first the great response that there has been by generations of charitably disposed persons to the call of the unfortunate of every kind, so that there are societies dealing with or attempting to deal with practically every sort of evil, physical or moral, and secondly, the vast amount of waste involved in the multiplicity of societies dealing with the same classes of people. Thus, a list of the institutions and societies dealing with the blind covers twenty-four pages. The effects of this multiplicity of societies will be dealt with later on in considering the general character of charitable work, but some description of different forms of charity is desirable.

PROVISION FOR THE SICK

Among our oldest charities are those making provision for the treatment of the sick, some hospitals even surviving from the Middle Ages. In mediaeval England the Guild and the Church were the two main organs of charity, both with a religious basis, and providing between them, to a greater or less degree, the various services later supplied by friendly societies or charities. The confiscation of the property of the Guild and the monasteries by Henry VIII. at the Reformation deprived society of the accustomed provision for the sick as well as for the poor and the homeless, for not only were the institutions suppressed, but the religious orders that made nursing one of their principal activities also disappeared. Very few survivals remain from this period, only a few hospitals, the most notable of which is St. Bartholomew's, founded in 1123, and our present hospitals are due in the main to the efforts of the charitable in the eighteenth and nineteenth centuries. Sickness, being one of the most usual of the accidents of life and one of the most potent causes of destitution, it is not surprising that the charitable should have given their money to provide for the sick, but the very slow recognition of the national importance of the health of the nation and the survival of the hospitals supported by voluntary contributions to our own day, may cause astonishment. We are, however, apt to forget how recent is the rise of medical science, and particularly of preventive medicine. The great extension of public provision for sickness to-day owes more to the advance of science and to the recognition of the social loss, occasioned by the withdrawal from work of many, and the loss of efficiency of others, than to the spirit of charity. The numerous hospitals that sprang up in the early part of the last century now stand out isolated from the general health service of the country in the same way as formerly they stood out amid the general lack of medical provision. It has already been mentioned that an unified health service for the whole country is now in process of formation, and the charitable worker will probably find better scope for his energies in working in connection with this service. There is, however, always need for specialised institutions, more particularly those of an experimental character, and while we may expect that in due course of time all hospitals will form part of the State service, it is probable that convalescent homes and rest homes will still remain in private hands. The free and provident Dispensaries, another form of charity that came into being in the eighteenth century for the provision of medical and surgical treatment and drugs for the poor, generally on the contributory principle, have also lost their usefulness owing to the passing of the Insurance Act. While the work of nursing may be considered in itself a social service, and the work of the village nurse in particular may have most valuable secondary effects in raising the general standard of health, the amateur can still find plenty of work to do. There are many people in hospitals who either have no friends or are far away from them, who can be visited, and for whom the loan of books, or gifts of flowers make a great deal of difference; among these may be mentioned especially the incurables.

In connection with many hospitals there are now appointed hospital almoners, whose duties are to assist the medical work by advice and instructions in following up treatment. This is a salaried post requiring social experience. The work consists principally in interviewing new patients after they have been seen by the doctor, and making inquiries as to their means in order to guard against the abuse of hospitals by those who are well able to provide medical attendance and treatment from their own resources. Also the almoners advise patients as to how best to carry out the instructions of the doctor, and how to obtain convalescent treatment, surgical instruments, etc.; in fact they follow up cases into the home and use all possible influence to ensure that the patient takes advantage of the advice given and obtains the means to regain health.

Among other societies providing auxiliary services to the sick may be mentioned the Invalid Children's Aid Society, which provides surgical appliances, etc., and supervises, by means of the personal visits of its members, the health of sick and crippled children.

An undesirable feature of some hospitals is a system of admission by tickets, given to subscribers of certain sums of money. Admission to an hospital should not be based on the favour of an individual but on the needs of the patient: still worse are those institutions, admission to which depends on securing a number of votes from subscribers. This system causes a great amount of wasted time and money in writing letters asking for support for a particular candidate, and success in the ballot is no guarantee that the candidate is the most deserving case, but only shows the energy of his or her supporters. This kind of thing serves to minister to the sense of self importance of people who like to feel that they have patronage at their disposal, and are, so to speak, getting value for the money subscribed.

The whole business of collecting for hospitals by special days on which collectors stand at the street corners and blackmail passers-by, or by which collections are made in factories, is thoroughly unworthy of the dignity of the service. Scarcely better is the system whereby large sums are given by persons who hope to receive titles in exchange ; there is no charity in the bulk of the giving to hospitals, and probably the only reason why this charity method of financing them continues is because of the unwillingness of the medical schools to put themselves in the slightest degree under the control of lay authorities.

MORALLY DEFECTIVE

A very important branch of charitable work is that which concerns itself with the endeavour to reform the morally defective. It is a sphere where the State cannot do so much as private persons, because the most important point is the personal influence brought to bear on the individual.

It is not the province of the State to deal with all offences against the moral law, but only with those which it for the time being regards as directly harmful to society, and though the idea of what these are may expand or contract according to the ideas of society at a given time, there will always be people who take a more extended view of what is socially dangerous than the majority. Thus sabbath breaking was at one time regarded as a serious offence against the moral ideas of the people, but is now reduced to an offence against the idea of the weekly rest day, and although the Lord's Day Observance Act is still on the statute book it is very seldom enforced. Again, although there are many people who regard drunkenness under any circumstances as a moral delict, it is not yet an offence punishable at law when indulged in quietly in a man's home. Thus there have sprung up many societies with the object of preventing moral offences or reforming those who are morally defective, or assisting those who have been punished for infringements of the law.

It is often said that you cannot make people good by Act of Parliament, and it is true, but you can lessen the temptation to go wrong or remove the cause of vice.

Thus, to take a case to which a very large amount of social effort has been directed, that of intemperance, it is not possible to make people sober by Act of Parliament unless you are prepared to go the whole way and prohibit totally the manufacture, sale and importation of intoxicating liquors as the U.S.A has recently done, but short of this there is much that can be done to remove the temptations to drunkenness and the opportunities for it. Public-houses may be reduced in number, kept open for a shorter period of each day, or rigorously inspected. Houses and conditions of labour may be improved, education extended, and counter-attractions provided which may all tend to reduce drunkenness by cutting at some of its causes. In this country there are voluntary societies working on all these various lines.

The direct method of attack is pursued by many societies that advocate total prohibition by State action, such as the United Kingdom Alliance. Less direct is that of the societies that try to work through the individual, by persuading him to sign a pledge to abstain from the use of intoxicants. Of these a large number are connected with the churches, while others, such as the Rechabites, form part of the Friendly Society movement.

Others again rely on the provision of counter-attractions and the reform of the liquor traffic itself. An example of these is the People's Refreshment House Association, which buys up public-houses and carries them on with the elimination of private profit on the sale of liquor and a high standard of management together with the provision of counter-attractions. Yet other societies confine themselves to endeavouring to reform those who are already victims of the habit by their reception into Inebriates' Homes, where scientific or spiritual methods or a combination of the two are employed to restore their moral.

CRIMINALS

Our present system of criminal justice looks to the punishment of offenders rather than to their reformation, to deterrence of others rather than the reclamation of the criminal, except in the case of juvenile offenders. The young offender is either committed to an industrial home or a reformatory, or is placed under the care of an officer of the court. These schools or reformatories are sometimes wholly maintained by local authorities, or are charitable institutions to which children are sent under the order of a magistrate, and they are partly supported by charity, partly by public money paid for the cases sent to them. This is a good example of the co-operation of voluntary organisations with the State whereby more flexibility is obtained, for there is room for experiment in new methods, and the devoted services of those interested in the work are secured. Under the Probation of Offenders Act young persons, instead of being sent to an institution, may be placed under a probation officer, whose duties are to keep in touch with the child and do all that is possible to keep him or her straight. It will be seen that the success of this measure depends entirely on the character of the person appointed to act as probation officer, some of whom are voluntary workers and others paid officials. It is a task requiring knowledge, patience and experience in dealing with very difficult cases.

In the case of adult offenders the societies deal chiefly with the discharged prisoner, endeavouring to influence him and to find him work. It is not generally realised how many of those committed to prison are more fools than knaves, and how many have now become irreclaimable criminals through the treatment accorded to them. Considerable light has been thrown on prison methods as a result of the imprisonment of a large number of qualified observers for political offences, especially the advocates of Women's Suffrage and the conscientious objectors. The majority of charitable societies deal with the deserving poor, and naturally do not touch discharged prisoners, who have a very difficult task in trying to regain their position, and to assist them to do so there are several Prisoners' Aid Societies and specialised departments of the Salvation Army and the Church Army. Mention must also be made of the Court Missionaries, to whom prisoners are handed over by the magistrates, especially in cases where the crime is obviously due to circumstances and not to a wilful desire to offend.

SEXUAL IMMORALITY

The prevention of sexual immorality is one with which the State is little able to deal directly save in the way of preventive measures against disorderly houses and the policing of the streets, and much of the work of protecting the inexperienced and endeavouring to reclaim the fallen is left to voluntary agencies.

The subject is a difficult one owing to the lack of straight thinking on the subject and the tendency to be satisfied with driving vice underground and pretending that it is non-existent, as well as to the general custom of wrapping the whole matter in secrecy.

The older charitable societies were apt to work too much on the lines of dealing only with the individual. They regarded sexual immorality as in the main a matter of the failings of the individual, and the only remedy his, or more usually her, conversion to a better frame of mind. Hence it is only recently that the causes of the prevalence of sexual immorality have been investigated from the social point of view. The intimate connection of prostitution with low wages of women has been recognised for some time, though it is sometimes pressed too far as a general cause, insufficient allowance being made for other factors; but what is not so generally recognised is the effect of the low wages of men.

Charitable persons have been apt to concentrate

their attention too much on one sex and ignore the other. There is no doubt, however, that much sexual immorality is caused by the low wages paid to many men which prevent early marriage. This does not operate so much in the case of the poorer classes, who usually arrive at their highest wages on attaining manhood, and to whom postponement of marriage is not likely to bring a better financial position, and to whom besides, marriage appears as a means of escape from an overcrowded home. But it is an effective cause in the classes above the poverty line with a comparatively high standard of life, whose wages or salary tend to increase as they get older; in their case postponement of marriage means a rise in the social scale, and among large classes of these the age of marriage is much later than in former times. If wages are one important factor another is housing, for where people are living in overcrowded conditions privacy is practically impossible, and the resulting effects are apt to be disastrous.

The problem is a very old one, and its solution appears to be a long way off, but it is doubtful whether the actions of the various societies engaged in rescue work are very fruitful of good; rather the attitude of moral disapprobation and the tendency of the churches to take a somewhat extreme and pharisaic attitude, together with their peculiar views on the divorce question, have rather tended to call attention away from less obvious causes than the sin of the ordinary man and woman. At the same time the value of the devoted work of the many rescue workers must be recognised, and the very great difficulty of their work appreciated: it is not work that everyone can do, or that very many are willing to undertake, and requires special qualifications. More hopeful, perhaps, are the societies which endeavour to protect those most exposed to temptation from themselves.

Though not directly and entirely intended for this work, societies such as the Girls' Friendly Society and the Metropolitan Association for Befriending Young Servants, in effect do much to protect the inexperienced. Working through local committees the societies aim at providing friends and advisers for young girls, especially for those in domestice service who are living away from their families and friends, and hostels also are established where single girls may live and be trained for domestic service. Staffed in the main by voluntary workers, these societies form a network of agencies all over the country to which the friendless girl or stranger can apply for advice and assistance, and also provide a form of club where the rather isolated domestic servant can meet others and have somewhere to go when free from work.

It is generally recognised that there is very much ignorance on sexual matters, and that this is one of the causes of the trouble. Comparatively little is done in any class of society to explain to young people the facts of life; the schools seldom touch the subject, and it is generally left to the parents, who are frequently unwilling to mention the subject. The Roman Catholic Church may be mentioned as an exception to the rule, and to this wise custom of instructing the young may be attributed the fact that sexual irregularity is less prevalent in that denomination.

An organisation that has done much good work is the National Society for the Prevention of Cruelty to Children, which operates through a number of paid inspectors who will investigate complaints as to the ill-treatment of children, and either warn the parents or those in control, or watch the case so as to intervene if necessary. The society prosecutes in bad cases, but its usefulness in this respect has on occasions been hampered by lack of sympathy from the magistrates, and as the few occasions on which it prosecutes without sufficient reason are more widely noted in the Press than those in which it is successful, with a bad effect on the support given to it, the society has to make very sure of its ground before taking action in the courts. The mere effect of a visit from the inspector is often enough to obtain improvement. School Care Committees make use of the society for difficult cases that are beyond the scope of the work of the school officials.

ORPHANS

The care of the orphan and the deserted child is one that has long gained the attention of the charitable; the Foundling Hospital, the Gordon Boys' Home, and the Waif and Strays, are examples of large institutions, but there are very many others supported particularly by the different religious denominations. The provision of these homes has been sometimes criticised as tending to weaken the sense of responsibility and encouraging loose sexual relationships, though the avoidance of this danger is especially aimed at by the latter society. It may be doubted whether the provision of homes for illegitimate children has much effect on the action of the parents, and the evil of leaving parents of illegitimate children to struggle to keep them while obliged to work for their livelihood is exemplified in the heavy death-rate among such children. In these homes an endeavour is made to train up the children for various sorts of work, particularly in the case of girls for domestic service.

There is always a difficulty in the case of orphans, when they go out to work, in providing for their boarding-out in suitable homes. It is generally undesirable from the point of view of the discipline of the institution and the children themselves to retain them in homes after a certain age; domestic service gets over the difficulty in the case of girls, and to meet the wants of others homes have been founded where young people can live and from which they can go out to work while a general supervision over them is maintained, so that those who took the responsibility of bringing them up can keep in touch with them. These homes are also utilised for children brought up in Poor Law schools. The Association for Befriending Boys undertakes for the payment of a small sum the supervision of boys who have left Poor Law schools and are out earning their living.

A well-known charity for the care of waifs and strays is that of Dr. Barnardo, who was impressed during his work in London by the large number of children sleeping out and homeless. His original work has developed to large proportions, with training and reception homes. A particular development has been that of emigration, more than 17,000 children having been emigrated to the colonies during the past forty years.

This policy of emigrating children is one followed by many societies and also by Boards of Guardians. As a rule the children are sent out while still young in order that they may grow into the habits of the country to which they are sent, and care is taken by inspection of the homes to see that those are suitable and that the children are well cared for.

Another opening for orphan boys is the sea service, either the Royal Navy or the Mercantile Marine. The first society to provide a training ship was the Marine Society, founded by Jonas Hanway in 1756, which is limited to boys of good character. Others that take destitute children are the Arethusa and Chichester, supported by the National Refuges for Homeless and Destitute Children, while some local authorities, such as the Metropolitan Asylums Board, have adopted this method of dealing with suitable boys in their charge.

The advantage of this method is the removal of the children from bad influences and the discipline of the life.

THE AGED

One of the commonest features of the English country town is the almshouses, the old buildings in a court with an inscription with the date and the name of the charitable founder, and until recently it was almost the only alternative to the workhouse. The founding of an almshouse was in fact one of the favourite ways whereby the successful man showed gratitude to the place of his birth or the town where he made his fortune. It was the custom for guilds and trades to found almshouses for the support of the aged and decayed members of the trade. Such are the Vintner Almshouses in Stepney, the Clothmakers in Islington, or the Merchant Venturers at Bristol. There are also a number of pension funds endowed or supported by societies or individuals for the benefit of the aged.

Despite the large number of these charities they have been wholly insufficient to provide for those unable to support themselves through old age, and for those who are helpless and have no relatives to look after them. Public opinion has gradually changed on the subject of old age, and it is generally recognised that there is no pauperism involved in State provision for those who have been worn out in industry. The provision by the Poor Law, always hated and dreaded as a deplorable ending to life by those whose penultimate resting-place was almost certain to be the Poors House, has now been superseded by the system of old-age pensions, although the amount is very inadequate. It may be expected that some form of almshouse will be set up for those who have no relatives to support them, and that in the future the almshouses, etc., carried on by voluntary subscriptions or provided by endowment will be linked up with the State provision under the pensions committee as a single service for the aged, controlled by voluntary committees, and partly supported from private funds, partly from subventions from the local authorities.

EDUCATIONAL CHARITIES

The conception of education as a fit subject for charity is one that is being replaced by that of the right of every child to receive at least elementary instruction, and the duty of the State to provide it. Yet this conception is modern, and for long education of every grade was looked upon as essentially a case for the action of individuals or religious bodies.

Thus there are still a large number of endowments

devoted to education in our grammar schools, public schools and universities. The foundation of schools was an act of charity frequently performed by monarchs, noblemen or by rich men, but although most of these foundations were originally intended for the poor, in course of time they have been diverted to the use of the well-to-do.

Some of these donations were prompted by zeal for education, others by a desire to benefit the place of the founder's birth, but most with the intention of promoting a particular form of religious belief.

Particularly is this the case with elementary education. At the beginning of the eighteenth century many schools were founded by the Society for Promoting Christian Knowledge in order to teach the doctrines of the Church of England, and the Sunday School movement that followed did more towards religious instruction than for purely educational work. The national schools of the Church and the British schools of the non-conformist bodies were partly instrumental for extending the influence of those bodies. It is a question whether the religious charities have done more to help than to hinder the cause of education.

On the one hand it may be claimed that charity stepped in and did work that the State was not at that time prepared to take up ; on the other, that the fact of its intervention delayed the foundation of a national system, and that its continuance, and the sectarian strife which accompanied it, did untold harm by diverting the interest of the people from essentials to mere squabbles of rival creeds. Credit, however, can be given to charity as the pioneer not only by the work of the societies already mentioned, but by such efforts as those of the Ragged School Union. To-day education offers an example of the way by which, in this country, institutions are adapted to new purposes. Instead of closing the voluntary schools, as has been done sometimes in countries where strife between clerical and anti-clerical has been acute, the denominational schools (now the non-provided schools) have been incorporated into the State system, retaining certain privileges, but losing others in exchange for State support.

After the State system of elementary schools had been created the work of charity was still found necessary, and found vent in the provision of meals—until this too was taken over by the education authorities and added to the system. Thus the whole sphere of elementary education has passed from charity, except in the case of a few schools carried on by special bodies or for special categories of persons, such as the blind, the deaf and the orphan.

Secondary education is still divided between private enterprise, municipal service and charity. Schools such as Christ's Hospital and many old foundations throughout the country, although they may contain scholars whose fees are paid by the rates, still draw their support largely from the charitable bequests of deceased benefactors which enable them to provide an education at a cheap rate.

If elementary and secondary education have passed or are passing from the position of charities to that of State services, there is still a very wide field for the exercise of charity in the domain of higher education. Compared with other countries, especially Scotland and the United States, the provision for university education is very insufficient in England, and the proportion of the population in attendance at universities insignificant. In the United States great charitable donations to universities constitute a not uncommon method adopted by the very rich to get rid of their surplus wealth, and although this has its own disadvantage in tending to make university teaching somewhat subservient to the millionaire, yet it does afford a great opportunity for benefiting present and future generations. That such donations are not more frequent in this country is due not to the lack of wealthy men, but to want of appreciation of the value of education. It is true that recently some business men are beginning to understand the importance of technical education, and that subscriptions can be obtained from them for endowing chairs of chemistry or commerce, but it is otherwise with those branches of knowledge that do not immediately subserve the interests of trade and industry. The endowment of research in this country is urgently needed, especially into economic and social conditions, and it is a little ironical that the principal endowment for examining into the causes of poverty should come from an Indian, not an Englishman. More important perhaps even than the provision of buildings or the endowing of professorships is the establishment of scholarships and bursaries, in order that university education may be open to those who are qualified to take advantage of it, instead of being confined, as it is to a large extent at present, to those who can afford it.

There is, too, plenty of room for pioneer work and experiment. The Working Men's College, Morley College, the Polytechnics and the University Extension Lectures, all owe their inception to the voluntary work and zeal for education of a few. New methods of teaching can be best proved by experiments on a small scale. If, for instance, the Montessori system were to be tested, it could hardly be done by a local education authority; it would not be fair that parents who were obliged to send their children to school should have to submit them to experiment. It could only be tried by getting a certain number of enthusiasts to send their children to a special school. New departures, such as the open-air school, and the school journey, required to be pioneered by private individuals, and all such experiments require not only work but money.

OPEN-AIR SOCIETIES

One of the most disturbing features of our society to-day is the separation of town and country and the steady increase of the proportion of the urban to the rural population. It is difficult for the ordinary person to realise how short a time man has been a town dweller, and how obscure are the effects of this on the human race due to the addition of so many other factors of industrial life. It used to be said that families living in towns died out in a few generations, though I have never been able to find any warrant for the statement, and the degeneracy of a town population seems to have been disproved by the war, where the men from industrial districts showed as much stamina as those from the rural areas. The fact remains, however, that the divorce of the bulk of the population from the country is a serious experiment, and that not only from the physiological, but from the social point of view.

The life of the town is especially unnatural for children, and tends to make their upbringing very one-sided. For instance, much stress is laid to-day on nature study, not only as a desirable branch of knowledge in itself, but also from its social importance in the easy opportunity it affords of teaching children the physical facts of life in a natural way; but even with the keenest teachers and the best apparatus it is hard to make this a living subject if children are segregated in towns, and hardly ever get out to the country. Again, much of the best in literature must be a shut book to the town dweller, unless from time to time he can get out to the country and appreciate nature. Thus one of the most useful forms of social effort is that which assists the town population to get out into the country.

A popular, but not on the whole very useful form of charity, is the Fresh-Air Funds raised by societies or individuals or sometimes newspapers, with the object of taking children from the slums of the towns for a day in the country or the seaside. It is better than nothing; but the time is far too short for much advantage to health or knowledge to be gained, and the fatigues of the journey and the long day frequently do more harm than good. Far more important are such societies as the Children's Country Holiday Fund, that arranges for children to be boarded out in country homes for a week or a fortnight. The London fund works through the schools, and arranges for the parents to pay weekly contributions to meet part of the cost, and inspects and finds the homes to which they are sent. This involves a large amount of detailed work, and there is always room for voluntary assistance in the summer months.

The summer camps for boys, and to a less extent for girls, are another means of getting the town child into touch with the country, though not in such an intimate way as when children are taken to live in families; it is the difference of seeing a foreign country from a hotel, or as so many have seen France, from a camp, and seeing it as a resident in a French family.

Of the various agencies providing camps, the best from the point of view of linking town and country is that of the Boy Scout movement. Like other extended movements, there is a good deal of variety in the characteristics of its various sections; some may be keen on the semi-military side of the work, others on the fresh-air side, and it is the latter that concerns us here. The movement is well designed to attract boys, with its combination of adventure, woodcraft, games and exercise, appealing as it does to the dreams of youth that are drawn so largely from the books of adventure, and gives great scope for the dramatic pose, whereby the dream almost comes true, while the underlying idea of duty and unselfishness lays the foundations of future good citizenship.

It is to be hoped that the extension of camping for adults that has already been tried with considerable success will be extended, some working-class organisations already have standing camps where their members can go for holidays, and if due encouragement were given there seems no reason why the movement should not spread.

I would like to see each urban area linked up with a rural one, affiliated, as it were, so that the country district should be in direct relation with the town, and that country people on a visit to the towns should stay with the town people in the same way as children are sent on country holidays. During the War the country was divided into coal-producing and coal-consuming areas, and each area of supply was allotted a consuming area: I would like to see this system extended so that a food-producing area should be brought into close touch with a certain district of food consumption, and that these two areas should mutually supply each other's defects of amenities. The town area would supply the country with its extra labour for hopping, fruit-picking and harvesting, and its schools for delicate children, its hospitals, etc., would be placed in that country area.

I believe that in this way a better understanding between the two would be reached by a mutual interchange of services, and that each could gain from the other so that the great gulf now existing between town and country might be bridged.

GENERAL CHARITIES

Besides all these societies specialising in particular groups of persons, or trying to supply specific needs, there is the mass of charity which consists only in supplying money or goods to the poor. A large number of them are nominally missions, but actually their energies are divided between begging and giving doles. Some advertise extensively the fact that every week they provide so many free dinners, or every winter supply so many blankets or tons of coal, or provide free lodging and supper for the homeless poor. This is perhaps the most useless type of charity. It is understandable that there may be occasions of national or local disaster when there is need for very large gifts of this kind, as in an earthquake or fire, or in the course of a great strike; but that societies should pride themselves on the fact that week in week out they make such distributions argues very little attempt to grasp the nature of the problems of poverty. These missions become centres of demoralisation and serve to add to the poverty of the district in which they are placed, for the district already possessed of a high percentage of people below the poverty-line finds itself swamped by an incursion of tramps, work-shys, and incorrigible beggars from other districts, who add to the housing difficulties and intensify the problems that the central or local authorities are trying to tackle.

Further, the knowledge that large sums are distributed has its effect on the wage conditions of the neighbourhood, in making the workers less ready to stand out for higher wages and employers less ready to give them, just as in towns like Portsmouth, with a large number of naval and military pensioners, wages tend to be lower than elsewhere, while very possibly the effect of the crowding-in of the demoralised to share in the doles causes the rents to rise so that the charity, far from being beneficial, is merely a subvention to the sweater and the slum landlord. If conditions are bad it is unwise to pretend that they are not, by providing a hand-to-mouth existence for the victims, who are thereby made less ready to take action on their own behalf.

Another class of dole-giver is the politician who wishes to ingratiate himself with his constituency. Especially is this true of the local politician whose object in getting on to a local body is to prevent action, for a little judiciously distributed charity is a cheap insurance against having his house property too rigorously inspected, or his public-house closed down. Besides these is the sentimental person who reads vivid accounts of the horrors of East London, and subscribes to these charities. The supply of money for charities is limited in actual practice, and there is a certain competition between charities for support ; and, just as in industrial life the sweated industry uses up some of the capital and labour that might be employed in sound businesses, so the useless or harmful charity competes with those that are really doing useful work for personal service and pecuniary aid. The true antidote to the harmful sort of charity is the better provision for all the needs of life and the prevention of the causes of poverty. Where actual poverty exists owing to low wages, sickness, unemployment or old age, it is impossible to condemn those who, though in an unfortunate manner, endeavour to relieve suffering, without more strongly condemning the indifference that does nothing at all.

WASTE AND OVERLAPPING

We can now see how large a field is covered by charity, and how great an amount of goodwill, personal service and money gifts are represented by it. In London alone the annual expenditure amounts to something near ten millions a year in the aggregate, and while we must recognise the amount of goodwill and social service that the charities of this country represent, we must also point out some of the drawbacks.

With so many societies working in the same field and acting independently, there is clearly a great deal of wasted energy and overlapping, and the fact that there is this large sum of money to be given away is likely to have a demoralising effect upon some people who will seek to make a living out of the gifts of the charitable.

Charity does not necessarily bless him that gives and him that takes. Very often it blesses neither the one nor the other. To avoid the dangers of charity good administration is necessary, and the co-operation of the various agencies, one with the other, in order to save waste and prevent imposture. Before dealing with the various efforts that have been and are being made to ensure these two desiderata, we must look a little closer into the working of the charity system, and we can best do that by looking back to the time when organisation, whether by private agencies or by State and municipal bodies, had not yet begun.

If recourse is had to the pages of "Punch," which always reflects the attitude of the bourgeoisie of the period very faithfully, one is struck in the volumes that appeared in the fifties and sixties of last century, by the number of portrayals of the beggar, and probably one of the things that would strike the prosperous citizen of that epoch if he were to return to life would be the very small dimensions to which that nuisance had sunk. In the fifties and sixties not only was poverty very great, but also pauperism, not so much the pauperism by a swollen Poor Law, but by the activities of the charitable societies and individuals.

The reasons for this state of affairs were many; first, the new Poor Law, although it reduced the number of those dependent on the rates and did something to prevent the demoralisation of the population, did nothing to stop poverty. Sickness and unemployment, the two great causes of poverty, were left to the individual to deal with; the public health agitation was but just beginning, unemployment was not recognised as a social disease but an individual delinquency. Those however who were brought into contact with the poor could not fail to find many hard cases, and to deal with these recourse was had to the pockets of themselves or their friends. From time to time reports of the bad conditions in poor districts would be brought to the well-to-do, and there would be a wave of sympathy, money would be collected and distributed, sometimes wisely, more often unwisely. Meanwhile, organised intervention by the State was ruled out, partly through the prevailing economic ideas, partly through lack of knowledge of causes, and partly through the idea that the Poor Law was all sufficient, and that if the figures of pauperism did not rise all was well. A good example of this latter idea, continuing even to the present time, is shown by the evidence of a Poor Law guardian before the Poor Law Commission, who stated that in his district applications for outdoor relief were rarely made and that people were getting their living without it, so that he concluded that their energy and industry had increased; whereas, in fact, a single charitable agency in the district was providing over 30,000 meals a year, besides distributing thousands of garments, boots and blankets, giving out hospital letters, and maintaining children in day nurseries. In the failure of the organised agency and the existence of distress it was inevitable for charity to step in and try to deal with the results of neglect.

The existence of this mass of competing and overlapping charities was not only ineffective and wasteful, but encouraged the cadger at the expense of the genuine poor, and gave the professional charity-monger the chance of exploiting the public sympathy by collecting for bogus charities or that type of institution in which management expenses vastly exceed the amounts given in charity, but provide a living for the exploiter. The evil of charity is that it tends to make the charitable think that he has done his duty by giving away some trifling sum, his conscience is put to sleep, and he takes no trouble to consider the social problem any further.

In any estimate of the value of charity in our social life the fact that the motive of doing a social service or an act of kindness is sometimes entirely absent and is overlaid with other motives must not be forgotten. Many give because it looks well to have their name on a list showing their importance or possibly their wealth, others because their help is solicited by some one with a title, or because they will have the chance of meeting Her Royal Highness. Others again, after a life spent in thoroughly unsocial actions, will endeavour to obtain absolution from the public by large well-advertised donations, whereby their previous activities will be forgotten, or perhaps they may get a title and thus conceal their previous identity.

Others again give through an uneasy feeling that things are not right, or from the hope that they are throwing a sop to Cerberus, *i.e.* the working-class, which will keep him quiet during their time.

It is unfortunate that there should be a certain *kudos* to be gained by giving in charity which is absent from the performance of a duty; thus a man will oppose any increase of taxation or local rates while he is prepared to give far more than these increases in charity. Very many do not realise that you must be just before you are generous.

As Bernard Shaw puts it, "Most of the money given by rich people in charity is made up of conscience-money 'ransom,' political bribery and bids for titles. The traffic in hospital subscriptions in the name of Royalty fulfils exactly the same function in modern society as Texel's traffic in indulgences in the name of the Pope did before the Reformation. One buys moral credit by signing a cheque, which is easier than turning a prayer wheel. I am aware, further, that we often give to public objects money that we should devote to raising wages among our own employees, or substituting three eight-hour shifts for two twelve-hour one's. . . . The mere disbursement of large sums of money must be counted as a distinctly suspicious circumstance in estimating personal character."

CHAPTER III

ORGANISATION OF SOCIAL WORK

IT has been shown in the last chapter how wide is the field of charitable effort and how numerous are the agencies at work, and some of the evils of overlapping and of indiscriminate and temporary relief have been indicated. If these evils exist to-day they were very much more prominent fifty years ago. The extension of local and central government into many new spheres of activity, particularly public health and education and the increased efficiency of municipal administration in general, has narrowed some spheres of unorganized voluntary effort and co-ordinated others, thus forming a framework within which voluntary action may operate. Increased education among the general public and a better appreciation of the causes of distress have reduced indiscriminate almsgiving and turned the attention of the charitable to the results of their actions.

In the middle of the nineteenth century, however, conditions were very different; investigation into social conditions was in its infancy, the technique of relief had not been developed, and the various forms of social service—which it is the object of this series to describe—were either non-existent or were represented by the uncorrelated efforts of individuals and groups of individuals. Despite the Poor Law reforms brought about by the report of 1834, pauperism was rife and begging common, and the Boards of Guardians—to which were assigned the duty of making provision for the destitute—differed widely in method and policy.

It was under these circumstances that the Society for Organising Charitable Relief and Repressing Mendicity, commonly known as the Charity Organisation Society, or more shortly the C.O.S., was founded. The main object of the society was the improvement of the condition of the poor by bringing about the co-operation between charity and the Poor Law, and between charitable agencies of all kinds, by spreading sound views on charitable work, creating a class of skilled almoners, and securing due investigation and fitting action in all cases, in order to stop pauperising and repress mendicity.

The founders of the Society realised that one of the principal evils of charitable work was the lack of system and the overlapping caused by numerous competing agencies. It was quite possible for designing persons to make a living entirely on doles from the Poor Law and from different charitable societies, getting sums of money from one, medical help from another, blankets and coal from a third, without any of the agencies concerned knowing what the others were doing. The proposed remedy was the formation of a central body to focus the charitable efforts in a district.

In furtherance of this idea committees were formed in the different districts of London, and it was hoped to get all those persons interested in the charities of a given neighbourhood to serve on these committees, together with representatives of the Poor Law Authority. The Society itself was not to be a relief society but a clearing-house for societies dispensing alms.

Thus, one charge commonly brought against the Society, that of expending tenpence on investigation and twopence on relief, is beside the mark, for, although the Society has in course of time come to administer a considerable amount of relief, that is not its primary purpose ; it is to organise and co-ordinate the activities of others.

The second point, that of spreading sound views on charitable work, is really the necessary basis of the first ; the Society wish to bring home to the charitable the effect on the recipient of their almsgiving. Charity has its twofold aspect—it is intended to benefit both parties, but concentration on the moral benefit to the giver is apt to have disastrous effects, especially in the case of casual doles of money or indiscriminate distribution of food. Unless some general principles of charity could be evolved and the general public educated in them it was useless to look for co-operation.

The third and fourth objects necessarily go together ; for if it is desired that charity should benefit the recipient his condition must be investigated in order to find out if he is really in need and what is the appropriate remedy. The endeavour of the Society to attain these objects resulted in certain principles being laid down. (1) Full investigation into circumstances. (2) No relief to be given unless it is adequate. (3) No relief to be given to hopeless cases. (4) All hopeless cases to be handed over to the Poor Law. How far have these objects been carried out ?

Taking the first point, that of organisation, it is

clear that great difficulties lay in the way, for the charities are not all actuated by the single motive of assisting those in distress; the largest number of them is connected with some religious denomination, and their primary object is the conversion of the individual to a particular creed. Free teas may be given not with the idea of feeding the hungry, but in order to collect a certain number of people together to listen to a religious exhortation. Other donations may be made to enhance the political popularity of a candidate for Parliament or some local body. Thus the C.O.S. was faced with a difficult task, and though it has achieved a partial success in uniting a good deal of charitable effort, yet its object is still far from realisation.

Two causes are especially responsible for this. One is the development of the C.O.S. committees into relief agencies, thus adding one more to those already in the field; this was almost inevitable, for as the society became known, charitable people who would not or could not take the trouble to do their own work entrusted it to the C.O.S., so that funds became available for the relief of selected cases. The other arose from the development of the Society into being the protagonist of a definite social creed with which many people could not agree. The strict division of cases into deserving and undeserving, or into Poor Law and non-Poor Law, was unacceptable to many who were inclined to doubt the validity of these categories and the scale of values upon which such discrimination was based; thus while the valuable idea of the organisation of charity owes much to the C.O.S., the actual grouping of social services and their coordination has increasingly become the work of the local authorities, and new societies, such as Guilds of

Help and Councils of Social Welfare, which have sprung into being to make a new attack on the problem, thus emphasising the failure of the C.O.S.

This failure was partly due to a rigid adherence to early ideas as to the sphere of State and voluntary action, and a general unwillingness to look beyond the Poor Law or to recognise the activities of the new and more specialised authorities as beneficial.

In educating the general public in sound views of charitable work the C.O.S. has done much, though their doctrine has been negative rather than positive; the evil of indiscriminate alms-giving is now far less than it was when the Society came into being, and there is a general recognition of its inutility; that this is so is to some extent due to the precept and example of the C.O.S.

No less important has been its influence on the training of the social worker and the development of a technique of investigation. The importance of thorough investigation into cases which it is desired to assist is impressed upon those who work under the Society, vague statements are discountenanced, and an endeavour is made to ascertain the genuineness of the case and the appropriate means of assistance. Details are inserted in case-papers so that the relevant facts may be immediately apparent to those who have to make decisions. The case-paper system, inaugurated by the C.O.S. and now used not only by charities but by Poor Law and other public authorities, facilitates uniform decision, provides for the compilation of records as to individual cases so that information can be transmitted to other agencies, and provides data for the compilation of accurate statistics. The local offices of the Society act as Bureaus of Registration so that a check can be placed on applicants by ascertaining from what sources they have been previously assisted.

By the introduction of system into charitable work much waste and overlapping has been prevented, and well-intentioned but ignorant people have been shown the danger of ill-conceived efforts and unthought-out remedies. Further, the system had led to the discomfiture of the professional beggar and the chronic cadger, and the Society may claim some of the credit due to the reduction of mendicancy. The principle that inadequate relief should not be given means that a very large proportion of applications will be rejected, but that those which are accepted will be dealt with thoroughly in such a way that the applicant will be tided over a period of temporary distress until he is once more self-supporting and on his feet again.

While the system of investigation introduced by the C.O.S. has been of great value, it has been accompanied by certain features that have militated against the success of the Society.

The fact that the Society is commonly used for the detection of impostors has led to the adoption of a tone of suspicion that runs through the work; a general assumption is made that all applicants are frauds unless they prove themselves otherwise, and this induces an attitude in the C.O.S. workers that is profoundly galling to the ordinary applicant, and is apt to bias those who receive their training from the Society. All social work is apt to be discouraging at times, and it needs a fairly robust faith in the general goodness of human nature to resist depression. It is my experience that the more trust is placed in a person the more he can be trusted, and that when once any one feels that he is suspected he will tend to be less straightforward than he would otherwise be.

The other feature is the general dislike that every one has to having his most private affairs made public. The art of collecting information requires not only thoroughness but immense tact in order to avoid wounding the self-respect of those who apply for relief: this tact is not always forthcoming, with the result that the applicant to the C.O.S. feels that he has to abandon all privacy and loses his self-respect. One ought constantly to remember how few of us would like to go through the ordeal of a full inquiry into our past history and that of our relations, and also that, although people may have applied for relief they have not necessarily lost this instinct of reticence, and if relevant facts have been concealed and are elicited with difficulty due allowance must be made.

It was inevitable that their actions would make the C.O.S. unpopular with the class that formerly lived on the charitable, the hopelessly demoralised and the professional beggar; unfortunately this unpopularity is found among all sections of the working class. Part of this is due to the somewhat harsh and tactless methods of some of the officials, still more to the general harshness of outlook and the peculiar social creed that has been adopted. As Canon Barnett once remarked, its members have a tendency "to clothe themselves in the filthy rags of their own righteousness." The attitude of complacency with the bourgeois code of morals and a certain lack of sympathy makes their charity a hard and unlovely thing, and the Society is regarded by the majority of the poor in much the same light as is the Poor Law.

In a paper read to the Society by Canon Barnett

in 1895 he pointed out that "charity was as disorganised and poverty as prevalent as in the year of the founding of our Society." After paying a tribute to the hard work and devotion of its members he traced its failure to "The Council having set up certain dogmas in the place of living principles, of narrowing the teaching which inspired its founders into a set of rules, and substituting a gospel fit for all times into laws which never grow. The C.O.S. did not lead public opinion and is not in sympathy with the forces of the time."[1]

Thus the C.O.S. has come to-day to hold rather a minor place in social service. Through its agency a certain number of individual cases of misfortune are relieved, a certain amount of co-operation between charities is secured, but in the main its functions are somewhat negative. It serves as a police force to the charitable to save them from being taken in by impostors, and is a convenient instrument for the making of enquiries, its organisation supplying skilled investigators and so saving time for those who are engaged in constructive work. It also provides a useful criticism on new schemes of social advance, with its continual emphasis on the importance of the individual and the family, an aspect of the social problem which in these days is sometimes in danger of being overlooked; but on the constructive side it is of little importance to-day, and few if any new experiments have been initiated by it, so that the more active social workers tend to pass it by and turn to more hopeful forms of activity.

The C.O.S. is primarily a London Society, but is in correspondence with Societies bearing the same or

[1] *Life of Canon Barnett*, by Mrs. Barnett.

similar names in the provinces that are organised on the same lines and adhere to a greater or lesser degree to the principles it maintains.

THE C.O.S. POINT OF VIEW

We have considered the C.O.S. as a Society and noted the scope and character of the work it performs; it is now necessary to consider the principles on which its members work and the attitude it takes up as a body towards social and economic questions. The Society is representative of a certain school of thought in social matters that has had in the past a large, and even to-day, has a considerable influence on public opinion.

Much of the criticism directed against the Society is, as has been shown, unjust, because it is based on the failure to understand its objects; but the more serious complaints are directed, not so much against its practical work as a Society but against its attitude towards social questions and the effect that this attitude has had on social progress.

In the first place the attitude of the school of thought represented by the C.O.S. is strongly individualist. It has little faith in any reform that is not primarily directed towards the reformation of the individual, and it holds that, in the main, the poor are poor because of their individual failings, and not through the defects of Society and its organisation as a whole. This attitude is an inheritance from the early days of the Society when the doctrines of the Manchester School were almost universally accepted by thoughtful people, and few Societies have ever remained so little affected in their attitude by the lapse of time, changed conditions and increased knowledge.

Secondly, and as a consequence of the first attitude, the Society holds that normally the family should be supported by the exertions of its head. As Sir C. S. Loch, the chief protagonist of the school states, "The head of the family must be responsible for providing against all the ordinary contingencies of life for himself, his wife and his children. However it be set aside in the pressure of existence this is the accepted position. If it be not accepted and acted upon the family will live under no strong and sturdy roof-tree but, whatever relief may be forthcoming, they will be liable to constant starvation and misery."

To this view is added the assumption that, as a rule, the ordinary man can obtain work, and that the work so obtained will provide him with a wage sufficient to keep himself and his family.

Thirdly, the Society, while approving of provision made voluntarily by groups of citizens through Friendly Societies, Co-operative Societies and Savings Banks for the supply of certain services, rejects all methods of provision that are made through the groups of citizens composing the State or the municipality, for they consider that this will have a pauperising effect.

Fourthly, recognising that there are occasions when help may be needed in exceptional cases, it believes that this is the sphere of charity. That for all the normal occurrences of life, sickness, old age, unemployment, funeral expenses, etc., the citizen should provide by mutual assurance the assistance of relations or some form of thrift, and that charity should only provide for the exceptional happenings. It does not consider that charity properly administered degrades, but that it fosters good feeling.

Fifthly, the Society has ever before it the dangers of pauperisation ; well acquainted with the Poor Law and its administration and sensible of the abuses connected with it, which were particularly great at the time the Society came into existence, it regards all extensions of State activity and communal provision of services through central or local government institutions as but extensions of the Poor Law. Old age pensions, school meals, unless paid for directly by the individual, are but extensions of outdoor relief and, together with such provisions as minimum wage regulations, tend to sap the independence of the poor and ruin the character of the working-classes. Especially dangerous does it regard all doles such as non-contributory old age pensions, that come to people without their working or paying for them, though this apprehension does not seem to extend to rents, interest and profits that come to the rich as the result of inheritance, chance, or by way of unearned increment.

Finally, this School takes its stand on the assumption that society as at present constituted is fundamentally just, that on the whole the distribution of wealth is not unfair, and that most people get what they deserve. Thus it decisively rejects all radical changes in the social or economic system, and looks for social advance to increased thrift, self-reliance and character on the part of the poor, and more thought and charity on the part of the rich. A typical instance of the C.O.S. position is exhibited in their attitude towards old age pensions, as explained by Sir C. S. Loch in "Aspects of the Social Problem." After discussing the causes of pauperism and reviewing the history of the provision made by the Poor Law, he considers the proposals put forward by the late Charles Booth for pensions of five shillings per week for the aged at sixty-five. He reviews the distribution of income between the various classes, showing that the wage-earning classes, though composing eighty per cent. of the population, only obtain forty-five per cent. of the National Income (at that date under £1 per week per wage-earner), and then estimates that old age pensions will cost something over twelve millions a year, which will be taken from the richer classes and be paid to the poorer. This means taking about £8 a year from the classes who average over £500 a year. The significance of these figures do not seem to strike him at all. He is concerned only with the danger of making paupers of people by holding out the enticing prospect of five shillings per week at sixty-five. Working men will spend their £1 a week in riotous living presumably because they are to get five shillings a week at an age to which few of them ever attain. To Sir Charles Loch, however, the matter appears in a terrible light. He fears it will kill natural affection among children and stop their willingness to support their parents. The transfer of the twelve millions will, he says, "create great and ruinous economic mischief and be a most fatal bounty. The money is now in the hands of those who, whatever their faults, are in the main desirous of turning the possession of it to the best economic account. It is money plus a certain intelligent energy in the holder, and transferred in a natural manner to others in payment for labour done it is no less, when thus transferred, the wage of intelligent energy in the receiver. But take it from the one class by the compulsion of taxation and hand it to the other for maintenance, and so far as it is a force for good and progress you devitalise it. Twelve millions a year less will be invested in trade by those who, as holders, have most interest in investing it well. Twelve millions a year will go to a single class, not as the result of their energy, but simply as a bonus, and also under conditions which require, neither directly nor indirectly, any return for the service rendered."

Sir Charles does not tell us what is the intelligent energy in the holder of railway shares or mining royalties, or why the money that goes to an old age pensioner is more of a bonus than that which goes to a landlord when his rents go up owing to pressure of population, or to a stockholder whose shares go up in the market.

To him the present distribution of income is the natural one; there are to him two classes, one which may only get money by working for it, the other, in whose interests he is particularly, though perhaps unconsciously, concerned, a class entitled to get money from property. Scouting the idea that the work of a lifetime has any social value, he lays down frankly the law of self-interest, that all work is done for the benefit of the individual—" We labour for ourselves." Hence he can see no justice in payments made to the worn-out veteran of industry, save perhaps a rough social justice. " In these taxation doles of five shillings there is no element that fosters good-feeling and gives life to the gift. Charity there is not, nor the reward of wages." The note of characteristic middle-class conviction that the present social system is based on justice is clear, and the assumption that charity does not degrade while State support does is most noticeable. Why the gift from a social superior should be considered less degrading than a pension from one's fellow citizen is not explained. Perhaps it depends on the amount. Five shillings a week at sixty-five degrades a workman, but two thousand a year to an ex-Cabinet Minister oı fifty thousand pounds to a successful general is apparently not degrading. This extract from Sir Charles Loch's article is not only interesting as showing clearly the attitude of mind of the Society, but also because the prophecies made therein as to the result of old age pensions have been so signally falsified in the result. The C.O.S. has always posed as being scientific, and at intervals lays down the law to poor ordinary mortals as to what they should do or forbear doing in a somewhat pontifical manner, and it is well therefore to call attention to their singular lack of prescience in this connection.

From this analysis of the attitude of the Society and from this extract from Sir Charles Loch's article, it will be seen that it is quite natural that a steady opposition should be offered by the C.O.S. to all tendencies making for increased control by the State. The point of view has its value in its emphasis on the fact that Society is composed of individuals, and that mere legislation cannot effect an entire reformation of conditions, unless there is also a reformation of the individual. The Society insists particularly on the importance of character: the question is what is meant by character, and it will have been seen that the points of character that are especially emphasised by the Society are those which are most convenient for the wealthier classes.

The C.O.S. is essentially designed for the defence of the propertied classes; the repression of mendicity a desirable thing in itself, the protection of the charitable from impostors, have always been among its chief aims, and it is quite natural that privileged classes should desire that working people should above all cultivate the virtues of sobriety, hard work and thrift ; a concentration by them on the possibility of individual success will tend to lessen the danger of inconvenient claims for a more equal distribution of the product of industry between capital and labour. The objection to communal provision for old age, sickness or unemployment, seems to be not that it is wrong that such provision should be made communally, but because the money will have to be provided in part from the pockets of the wealthy.

It is curious that the assumption that the ordinary working man can provide out of his wages for the ordinary contingencies of life, should continue to be the basis of the Society's social philosophy despite all the evidence accumulated by the investigations of Mr. Rowntree and the late Charles Booth, not to mention official enquiries, showing that a very large number of workers do not earn sufficient to provide even the bare necessaries of life. Hence to the modern reader of Sir Charles Loch's article the immediate suggestion would occur that, given his position, the obvious thing to do would be to consider how wages could be raised in order to allow the working man to support his family, and one would have expected that C.O.S. members would have been strong supporters of the demands of the organised workers for higher wages, but they have never shown any enthusiasm for Trade Unions except as thrift organisations. This is due to their obsession with the individual and their general outlook, which is, to put it bluntly, that "the poor in a lump are bad."

The high social value set on charity by the Society

has been already noticed, and is well brought out in the proposals of the majority of the Poor Law Commission of 1909, where the suggestion is made that those in need of relief should be passed through a sort of sieve, the more deserving being dealt with by charity, the less deserving by the Poor Law. I consider that charity is infinitely more degrading than public assistance when that charity comes from those in a superior economic position. Charity is only possible without loss of dignity between equals. A right established by Law, such as that to an old age pension, is less galling than an allowance made by a rich man to a poor one dependent on his view of the recipient's character and terminable at his caprice. Thus the right to receive an income from the ownership of property guaranteed by law has not apparently proved very degrading to those to whom it is conceded. On the other hand the unemployed cry of "Damn your charity, we want work," was a profound protest against the idea that charity is a substitute for justice.

It is curious that people of this School, while denying that men and women can be made good by Act of Parliament, should have so great faith in the possibility of promoting morality by charitable gifts. The whole system of organised charity rests on the conception that it is possible to divide the sheep from the goats, and that if the deserving poor are encouraged by charity the goats will become more like sheep in the hope that they may pass into the category of the deserving. Hence assistance will be given to those who show signs of thrift or are not addicted to drink, or have not offended against sexual morality, and the refusal of relief will be used as a lever to make parents look after their children by the very people who will object to the power of the law being used to prevent sweated wages being paid or high rents exacted.

Another result of the point of view of this school of social workers is that they are prone to consider the working man or woman as members of a distinct class, and not as ordinary human beings with the same desires and the same capacity for a full life as anybody else. Thus they will elaborate the number of economies that can be effected by the careful; how abstention from the consumption of alcohol or tobacco will leave more money for necessaries.

They will inveigh against expenditure on luxuries, the purchase of a piano by a working man outrages their sense of what is fitting, and they will spend much time in finding out ways in which small wages may be made to go a long way without considering whether those wages should not be raised, or recognising that the claim to a share in the better things of life which is expressed by the purchase of luxuries is a more hopeful thing than submission to low wages, and the careful cultivation of thrifty habits. In the same way every endeavour will be made to induce relatives who are just above the border line of poverty to pinch themselves to support an aged relative without considering whether it is really desirable in the interests of society as a whole, that the poorest classes of the community should be saddled with the burden of keeping not only themselves but their relatives in order to spare the pockets of the rich.

The whole cause of the inevitable failure of charity organisation is admirably put by Robert Louis Stevenson in his essay on beggars: "Gratitude without familiarity, gratitude other than as a nameless element in a friendship, is a thing so near to hatred that I do not care to split the difference. Until I find a man who is pleased to receive obligations, I shall continue to question the tact of those who are eager to confer them. What an art it is to give even to our nearest friends! and what a test of manners to receive! How upon either side we smuggle away the obligation, blushing for each other; how bluff and dull we make the giver; how hasty, how falsely cheerful the receiver. And yet an act of such difficulty and distress between near friends it is supposed we can perform to a total stranger and leave the man transfixed with grateful emotions. The last thing you can do to a man is to burthen him with an obligation, and it is what we propose to begin with! But let us not be deceived: unless he is totally degraded to his trade anger jars in his inside and he grates his teeth at our gratuity.

"We should wipe two words from our vocabulary—gratitude and charity. In real life help is given out of friendship or it is not valued; it is received from the hand of friendship or it is resented.

"Here then is the pitiful fix of the rich man; here is the needle's eye in which he stuck already in the days of Christ and still sticks to-day, firmer, if possible, than ever: that he has the money and lacks the love which should make his money acceptable. . . .

"And yet there is one course which the unfortunate gentleman may take. He may subscribe to pay the taxes. There were the true charity, impartial and impersonal, cumbering none with obligation, helping all. There were a destination for loveless gifts; there were the way to reach the pocket of the deserving poor, and yet save the time of secretaries! But, alas! there is no colour of romance in such a course; and people nowhere demand the picturesque so much as in their virtues."

The whole essay should be carefully read and considered by all those who are about to take up any form of relief work.

ORGANISATION OF SOCIAL WORK BY OTHER VOLUNTARY AGENCIES

The failure of the C.O.S. to organise charity has led to the formation of other organisations on a broader basis, notably Councils of Public Welfare, Civic Leagues and Guilds of Help. Here and there too, some particular society, owing to the presence of a particular individual, will undertake the organisation of a district, a Settlement, a Branch of the Invalid Children's Aid Association, or perhaps some active minister of a religious denomination will, through the strength of his personality, form a focus around which all the ameliorative activities of a district will centre. The aim of the Council of Public Welfare and the Guild of Help is not merely to co-ordinate the charitable work of a district, but to form public opinion and promote good citizenship, acting as it were as the conscience of the district in social matters. The Guild of Help movement has many points in common with the Elberfeld System in Germany in its insistence on the need for every citizen to do his part in promoting social well-being, and in its endeavours to get the ordinary citizen to collaborate in social work with the local authorities. Their endeavour is to get all those who are interested in social work, or in the civic life of the district, from whatever class they may be drawn, to combine together, to use the forces at their command in co-operation, so as to prevent overlapping, to enlist everybody that can be obtained in actual social work, and to make investigations into conditions and suggestions as to reforms needed.

The objects of the Guild of Help have been defined as follows:—" First: to deepen the sense of our responsibility for the poor and to promote through personal service a neighbourly feeling among all classes of the community. Second: to provide a friend for all those in need of help and advice, and to encourage them in efforts towards self-help. Third: to discourage indiscriminate alms-giving by private persons, and to organise methods whereby the generosity of such persons may be usefully directed, and enabled to secure results of permanent benefit. Fourth: to co-operate with all-existing charitable agencies in order to prevent overlapping. Fifth: to arrest the inroads of poverty in its initial stages in order to prevent the poor from sinking into destitution, and to ensure as far as possible that no home shall be broken up which can be saved by friendly advice and assistance. Sixth: to consider the causes of poverty in the town and to bring influence to bear, through public bodies or by private effort, to lessen or remove them." These aims might at first sight appear to be just the same as those of the C.O.S., but the fact of the Guilds arising long after the older Society had been in the field, points to some radical difference; this is, in the main, a difference of outlook, of spirit rather than of outward form. The Guild of Help aims at being more democratic than the older organisation, which, as has been shown above, is distinctively middle-class, and has come to represent a definite social creed, and a somewhat antiquated outlook.

The C.O.S. is to some extent a highly trained instrument for the protection of the charitable, the Guild of Help lays more stress on the enlisting of every possible volunteer in social work, and especially insists on the personal services of its members. Where the C.O.S. enables the charitable to bestow their money through its agency without the trouble of personal investigation, the Guild of Help insists upon the importance of the personal services of the donor in the bestowal of his gift. Again the C.O.S. is not much inclined for co-operation with the State outside the rather narrow range of Poor Law, while the Guilds are less influenced by the fear of extensions of municipal services leading to pauperisation.

In the fifth of the objects of the Guild set out above, the idea of anticipating the falling of a family into destitution is strongly insisted on, whereas the C.O.S. have always laid much stress on the deterrent idea, and its endeavours have always been directed not so much to the relief of poverty as to prevent applications for relief being made. The sixth object suggests that the Guilds are free from over-emphasis of individual shortcomings as causes of poverty, and are inclined to take their part in investigation and experiment. In fact it may be said that the Guild of Help represents the social service ideal where the C.O.S. represents the charity tradition. Councils of Public Welfare, Civic Leagues, etc., are much the same as the Guilds of Help, but the latter particularly insists on an adequate representation of organised labour on its executive and principal Committees. There is always a danger that these organising societies will become too exclusively middle-class, and this danger is guarded against in the constitutions of the Guilds of Help. Other organisations that may be mentioned are the various Federations of Boys' and Girls' Clubs which aim at spreading useful ideas among the different Club managers, preventing competition for members and arranging for joint activities wherever possible, such as inter-club contests in cricket, football and other forms of athletics. Recently the Home Office has set up Juvenile Organisations Committees with the object of co-ordinating the various agencies dealing with recreation for children and young persons. The control of these has now been transferred to the Board of Education.

Societies have been formed such as the Cavendish Association, and the Personal Service Association, with the principal aim of recruiting voluntary workers and sending them to those spheres of work where their services are most needed.

THE ORGANISATION OF SOCIAL WORK BY THE STATE AND MUNICIPALITY

Besides the organisation of voluntary social work by various Societies, there has grown up during the past half century a Municipal system that touches so large a part of the field of social service that some account of its structure is desirable. It may be said that the local governing authorities are to-day the principal instruments for the organisation of social work.

The old school of social workers were accustomed to look to the Poor Law authorities as the principal expression of State care for the poor, and formerly in a social series a book devoted to an explanation of

Poor Law principles and Poor Law work, would have been included. To-day the Poor Law system, already much diminished in importance through the transfer to other agencies of various classes of persons who formerly came within its purview, is under sentence of death; the various activities of the Boards of Guardians are to be transferred to other authorities, and it is only necessary here to give a general outline of its principles in order that references to it may be understood. Its particular functions with regard to different classes, the sick, the aged, the feeble minded, and the unemployed, will be dealt with in the books of this series devoted to those subjects as forming a part only of the provision made for them in the past. It is therefore not intended to give the history of the Poor Law in any detail in this place, but to indicate the principles on which it was based which have had great influence on social policy, and to explain its organisation.

The Poor Law then takes its rise from the Act of Queen Elizabeth's reign whereby parishes were to make assessments for the support of the poor with the general idea that the poor should be put to a useful and remunerative work. The causes which produced this Act were the fact that at the Reformation the old mediaeval system whereby the Church, and particularly the monastic orders, were in the main responsible for the poor, was swept away, and also the changes produced at the same time by the first enclosures and the introduction of sheep-farming, which caused widespread distress, and necessitated some new form of social machinery to cope with them. During the eighteenth century the habit of giving pecuniary relief to the poor had the effect of wholesale pauperisation of the population, particularly in the rural areas where Poor Law relief grew into a regular supplement to wages, with the result that not only were wages reduced to a very low level, but practically none but those in receipt of allowances from the parish could get work. It is unnecessary here to describe the state of affairs due to indiscriminate out-door relief, or to the effect of the law of settlement on the economics of the country side. It was ended by the Poor Law Commission of 1834, and future legislation and administration were based on the principles laid down therein.

In brief outline these principles were, that relief was for the destitute, not for the poor; that the condition of the pauper must not be made more eligible than that of the outside worker, and that the Poor Law must be deterrent, that is to say, that the aim of its administration must be to prevent people obtaining assistance. The principal method whereby this was to be effected was by the abolition as far as possible of all relief given to people in their own homes, and the offer instead to take them into the workhouse, which was to be a place that would not be willingly entered by anyone. The various categories of persons under the Poor Law were to be segregated into separate Institutions, and the Poor Law was to be administered by elected persons, while the Administrative Unit was extended from the parish to the Union of parishes. The immediate effect was a great reduction in the number of paupers, accompanied by an intense unpopularity of the new Poor Law among the labouring classes, which has lasted to the present time. It is important to remember that these principles were adopted to deal with a very definite state of affairs, that of the wholesale pauperisation of the working classes and were based on the assumption that the old Poor Law was the cause of much, if not of all, of the prevailing poverty, and that once the system of doles had been abolished the normal man would be able to gain adequate subsistence for himself and his family through his own exertions; the Poor Law was to be only for the destitute, and there was no intention of using the power of the State to help the poor or to raise the standard of life.

It was also intended to deal, in the main, with the pauperisation of the able-bodied, and Poor Law institutions were to be divided into sections for the able-bodied, the aged, the sick, etc. The failure of the Poor Law was due to a number of factors, the chief of which was the failure to realise that poverty and destitution were normal incidents of the modern industrial system, and that in the absence of any possible way of finding out whether a man was, for instance, unemployed through his own fault, or through circumstances out of his control, it was impossible to enforce the Workhouse test. Further, despite the proposed classification of paupers, in practice the general mixed workhouse continued, and it was impossible to enforce strict administration on the different categories of persons thrown together under a common roof. And despite the principles of 1834, outdoor relief persisted. Above all, the Poor Law did nothing to prevent destitution arising, but only dealt with it after it had arisen. It dealt only with results and not with causes; thus whether the administration was strict or lax there remained year in and year out a great body of persons who were suffering from poverty, although not assisted by the Poor Law.

It is unnecessary to labour this point of the failure of the Poor Law, for it is shown by the fact that other agencies have had to step in and do the work which from its very nature a destitution authority was unfitted to perform. Wherever it was attempted to enforce strict administration and to deter applicants from coming to the Poor Law, missions, soup kitchens, night shelters, and other charitable Institutions sprang up. Charity, whether organised or unorganised, whether working in conjunction with the Poor Law or against it, failed entirely to solve the poverty problem.

In course of time there arose a series of new authorities based on prevention rather than cure, which attacked the problem from a different angle. Thus the medical side of the Poor Law could not extend as its services were confined to the destitute, but the public health authorities in town and country originally formed for sanitary purposes have gradually extended into all sorts of activities dealing with the prevention of the origin and the dissemination of disease. Another invasion of the medical side of the Poor Law was brought about by the National Health Insurance Act, and at the present time we are well on the road to a unified public health service.

In the same way the education authorities have had to extend their functions from dealing with the minds to dealing with the bodies of their children, supplying school meals and medical treatment, and in some cases residential schools. The care of persons of unsound mind was gradually transferred, as to the greater number of such persons, to the Asylum Committees of the County and County Borough Authorities, while a realisation that the Workhouse was no fit place in which the worn-out slaves of industry should finish their lives led to the passing of the Old Age Pensions Act. Finally, the able-bodied man, who was particularly the subject of the Poor Law, is now looked after to a great extent by the Central Government. Unemployment is recognised as a disease of industrialism; the Unemployed Workmen's Act was entrusted to the local authorities other than the destitution authorities, and later attempts at prevention of unemployment by the establishment of employment exchanges and unemployed insurance were further examples of a passing by of the Poor Law authorities, and the creation of new machinery to deal with the able-bodied. Thus, throughout the country there were rival authorities dealing with the same groups of people, the one in so far as they were destitute, the other in accordance with their various needs. At the present time, as is indicated in the Ministry of Health Act, it is proposed to abolish the Poor Law as an unspecialised service dealing with the destitute, and split up its functions among the other authorities, thus adopting in the main the lines of reform laid down by the minority of the Poor Law Commissioners of 1909. Owing to its nature and the principles upon which it was based it was impossible for the Poor Law Authority to form a nucleus round which might gather the charitable efforts of a neighbourhood, nor owing to its principles and the fact that its areas cut across the other lines of local administration, could it be linked up with new authorities. It could only be the last resort of the destitute, and its fundamental principle of deterrence prevented it from becoming part of any movement for the extension of the activities of the organised community to the communal provision of services necessary to its welfare. On the other hand the growth in the activities of local bodies and the constant extension of the work of their various committees into spheres of work that were formerly considered the particular preserve of charitable and voluntary associations make it admirably fitted to be a centre for all kinds of social work. This does not mean that there is not room for groupings of voluntary workers in such organisations as the Guilds of Help, but that these associations will more and more take up the attitude of assisting by personal service the operation of the organised community. Instead of being, as in the C.O.S. conception, an alternative service to that of the State or Municipality, worked on different principles, and considered to be more favourable to the individual, the Guild of Help will seek rather to assume partnership in the undertakings of the local authority, supplementing the paid official with the personal service of the volunteer.

As the local authority has now become the chief agency for the organisation of social work the voluntary worker is continually being brought into contact with its various activities, even where he is not actually working in close co-operation, so that it is necessary to have a clear idea of the general organisation of English local government. A detailed examination of the work of the local council will be dealt with in this series in the separate volumes devoted to particular subjects, and it will be enough in this place to give an outline of their general structure.

1. The parish council or parish meeting. This is the smallest authority with which the social worker may have to deal, and its importance, except for certain financial purposes, is confined to rural areas.

Its powers are very limited, not only because large duties have not been given to it, but because its financial resources are very small. It can maintain footpaths, provide recreation grounds and allotments, and divides powers of housing with the larger authorities. In some parishes the council has actually erected houses, but the procedure is very cumbersome, reference having to be made to the rural district and the County Council, so that these powers have not been widely utilised. Under the various adoptive acts it can provide baths and wash-houses and libraries, and make arrangements for street lighting.

There is considerable scope for the active social worker in a village by using the powers of the Parish Council to make the village a brighter and more cheerful place. Although the financial resources of the parish are very small, yet there is no reason why, where enthusiasm has been aroused, the inhabitants themselves should not make such things as recreation grounds, and village institutions.

2. Municipal Boroughs, Urban Districts and Rural Districts between them divide the area of the administrative county, and are authorities of much the same type but with a diminishing scale of powers. The Rural District Council, within the area of which are the parish councils already mentioned, is in the main a sanitary authority, though it has powers under the Housing and Town Planning Act, and the Highways Acts. The Rural District Council is composed of the same members as the Board of Guardians for the area. The Rural District Council as a rule is not very active, for in a scattered country district there are not so many services that can be conveniently run by a local authority. The Urban District Council,

in addition to the powers of the Rural District and the power of putting into force the adoptive acts mentioned in connection with the parish, can also undertake municipal trading, such as waterworks, tramways, gas or electric lighting, baths, markets, etc. The Urban District may range in size from a mere country village to great towns of the size of Willesden or Rhonddha, with over 150,000 inhabitants, and the undertakings which they carry on will vary according to their size and the needs of the district. Urban and Rural District Councils are composed of elected representatives presided over by a Chairman.

The Municipal borough, consisting of a Mayor, Aldermen and Councillors, has the powers of an Urban District Council, and in addition may have ancient powers derived from charters or local acts of parliament. Some of them have considerable property. Doncaster, for instance, owns its race course, and Colchester its oyster fisheries. Urban District Councils with over 20,000 population are local authorities under the Education Acts, the Old Age Pensions, the Shops and National Insurance Act, and where the population is over 50,000 they are authorities under the Unemployed Workmen and Naval and Military Pensions Acts. The Municipal borough with 10,000 inhabitants is the education authority, and has powers in relation to weights and measures, food and drugs and police. And that with over 20,000 inhabitants is the local pensions authority.

3. The County borough stands for purposes of administration outside the geographical county in which it is situated, and is the most complete of all the local authorities combining the powers of the county council and the municipal borough. It is ruled

by the Mayor or in some cases the Lord Mayor, Aldermen and Councillors.

4. The Administrative county which is not necessarily coterminous with a geographical county, is governed by a Chairman, Alderman, and Councillors, and its most important powers are (*a*) Sanitation in conjunction with the smaller authorities, (*b*) Housing and town planning, (*c*) Highways and bridges, (*d*) Police, (*e*) Education, (*f*) Licencing, (*g*) Unemployed workmen and old age pensions, (*h*) Small holdings and allotments.

This then is the general structure of local government in England and Wales outside London, which has a peculiar system of its own.

In London there is a County Council consisting of a Chairman, Aldermen and Councillors, with duties and powers much the same as those of a county borough, with the exception that it divides its powers with certain minor authorities and with *ad hoc* bodies indirectly elected controlling areas sometimes equal but sometimes greater than that of the county.

The City Corporation, although represented on the L.C.C. is in the main independent of it, and consists of Lord Mayor, Aldermen, and Councillors, who are chosen according to the ancient constitution of the city.

The remainder of the County area is divided between twenty-eight Borough Councils each consisting of Mayor, Aldermen, and Councillors, which are mainly sanitary authorities, though also charged with the ordinary duties of provincial borough councils, such as lighting, housing in concurrence with L.C.C., the provision of libraries, baths etc.

The Metropolitan Asylums Board, which is indirectly

elected by the Boards of Guardians, is really a public health authority responsible for the provision of isolation hospitals, asylums, ambulance services and training ships. The Metropolitan Water Board consists of representatives of the London County Council, the Metropolitan Borough Councils and the City and certain extra-London authorities, and administers the water supply of greater London, which was formerly in the hands of companies. London Police, except in the City, are under a Commissioner appointed by the Home Office, while the Thames Conservancy, Port of London Authority, and Central Unemployed body, are other examples of *ad hoc* bodies variously composed and dealing with certain specific services.

All these authorities, except the parish, work on a system of committees to which different branches of the Council's work are remitted, and in practice the most important part of the work is transacted on committees and not in full meeting. The number of committees and their character will depend on the size of the authority and the powers which it has. The County borough is the most complete authoiity in the country, but though in county areas the powers are divided between greater and smaller bodies, from the standpoint of the social worker an examination of the work of a county borough council will show the range and extent of the operations of municipal bodies and the division of services between the committees.

Thus the public health committee is responsible for the prevention of disease and the removal of the conditions that cause it, the cleanliness of the streets, collection of refuse, inspection of food and houses, protection of infant life. Further it is responsible for the treatment of those suffering from infectious diseases so that it has a hospital authority sometimes on a large scale. The impending transfer of the Poor Law medical service to the public health authority promised in the Ministry of Health Act and the probable transfer of the function of the local Insurance committees will make these committees responsible for the organisation of all the health services in their districts, though the treatment of school children may remain under the education authority. The Asylums committee making provision for all varieties of the feeble-minded may be regarded as a specialised branch for the treatment of the sick. Whatever adjustments of areas and authorities may be made it is clear that there will be in each area an unified service for the prevention and cure of disease, and it is inevitable that all charitable work for the benefit of the sick will tend to be grouped around it, supplementing but not attempting to rival it.

While the direct attack on disease is led by this committee, there are others that assist less directly, especially some of these dealing with trading undertakings. Baths and wash-houses, parks and open spaces, water supply, all play their part, though under separate committees.

Again the Education Committee takes for its field the life of the child, and here the transfer of Poor Law schools will enlarge its functions, the number of residential schools under its care being much increased. Orphanages, institutional schools, training-ships, and charities of a like nature will find their functions in providing for the varied demands of different classes of children. Probably in time the clubs, scouts etc., will increasingly take the school for their centre, particularly as the extension of the period of school life will deprive them to some extent of the chief subject for charitable work of this nature, viz., the boy of fourteen or fifteen in a blind alley occupation.

The housing question is now recognised as too great for solution by the individual, and the housing reformer's best opportunity is on his local housing committee.

The Pensions Committee again will be the centre for all work with the aged, and will probably undertake not merely the payment and the investigation of the condition of persons who are able to look after themselves, but will have to undertake the provision of alms-houses by itself, or in conjunction with voluntary agencies, for those who need care and attention.

With regard to the able-bodied, it seems certain now that the provision made for the unemployed will be mainly through the State authorities. Our present system of Labour Exchanges is very far from perfect, and the co-operation of voluntary workers who will think out plans to make them more efficient and to link them up with voluntary agencies for training workers for new industries or for work on the land will be very valuable. This assistance is at present largely confined to the Juvenile Advisory Committee. As we have come to recognise that the problem of unemployment in its wider issues can only be dealt with by attacking causes that lie deep in our present industrial system, so at the same time it is important not to lose sight of the fact that we have, at present, men and women who are the victims of that system, but who need remedial efforts applied to them as individuals before they can again take their place as citizens, and as useful industrial units. It is this individual attention that can be best supplied by the voluntary worker.

Thus we can see that to-day while the need for the organisation of voluntary work is as necessary as it ever was, the changes of conception from charity to social service has rendered it necessary to organise effort on rather different lines from those previously laid down, and that to-day the greatest unifying force is now that of the local governing body, and that social workers regard themselves less as philanthropists doing kindly acts than as citizens fulfilling their duties.

CHAPTER IV

SOCIAL SERVICE IN CONJUNCTION WITH CENTRAL AND LOCAL GOVERNING AUTHORITIES

OUR citizens attend both to public and private business and do not allow their absorption in their own various affairs to interfere with their knowledge of the city's. We differ from all other States in regarding the men who hold aloof from public life not as quiet but as useless, so run the words of Pericles' Funeral Oration. "Democracy involves," says Mr. Zimmern, commenting on this passage, "the co-operation of a large number of citizens in the actual work of government: it means payment to the Government not only in taxes but in time and thought. Rich Athenians gave free gifts of money for ships, choruses, or public monuments: poor Athenians (and they were mostly poor) gave their widows' mite themselves."[1] He goes on to point out how large a number of the citizens of Athens took part in public business, and how much time and trouble it involved.

Thus it was in Athens during its best period, and thus too it was in the city States of the middle ages, in Florence and Genoa and in our own cities, but thus emphatically it is not in England to-day.

[1] *The Greek Commonwealth*, A. E. Zimmern.

The proportion of men and women taking an active share in civic life is very low, and even the proportion of those who take an intelligent interest in the affairs of the city, the county, and the State, with an appreciation of the issues raised by the various policies propounded, is not large. During the European War, it is true, almost every citizen was called upon to give his personal services to the State (though not his money, this was only loaned) either as a soldier or as a civilian, and numbers of those who had formerly considered only their own affairs were drawn into war work of one sort or another. But there does not seem to be very much reason to expect that this giving of personal service to the community will be carried on into peace time, unless the same kind of enthusiasm can be aroused. The menace of a great danger called out unsuspected reservoirs of devotion and effort, but it will be difficult to make people realise that the danger to civilisation has not passed away, though German Militarism has been beaten in the field; yet the dangers to civilisation are still very great, and the enemy is the apathy and lack of public spirit of the ordinary citizen.

It is, of course, far easier for public spirit to be evoked in a small community where everybody knows everybody, just as a small political or religious community is able to keep the fire of enthusiasm among its members alive through the mere fact of its diminutiveness and isolation; and it is the great size of modern communities that constitute the biggest difficulty in the way of creating and quickening a public spirit.

Again: the great complexity of modern life, the difficulty of understanding the underlying causes of events, and the interaction of various forces, make the position of the modern citizen very different from that of the Athenian. It is difficult for the ordinary citizen to grasp world politics or even national politics. How shall the man in the street find time or means to estimate the rights and wrongs of the quarrel of the Poles and the Tczecho-Slovaks over the Teschen district ? or decide for or against the nationalisation of a public service ? or appreciate the factors involved in a rise or fall in prices ? He may have an opinion based on such materials as he can lay hands on, and he may decide certain questions on *a priori* principles, but he does not know from personal experience enough of the question at issue to be able to decide properly on its merits.

Again in municipal affairs, there are many factors that militate against good citizenship—the migratory habit—the featureless wastes of dwellings that are in no sense cities, but merely dormitories: there is little to distinguish between suburbs like Tottenham, Ealing, or East Ham; how can a civic pride and interest in them be evoked ? There is, too, the fact that the modern citizen's interests are dispersed over a far wider area than was the case in the ancient world, where the city was the religious as well as the civic centre, and where art and amusements were also civic matters. But making allowance for all these factors, it is at bottom really a false outlook based on a mistaken philosophy that accounts for the limited amount of interest in public affairs.

The old individualist attitude of regarding the State as a sort of policeman to be ignored as much as possible may be dead, but its effects still endure in the curiously detached attitude that many people take up towards political and civic life. Many men take an odd sort of pride in this detachment from

G

political life of the same kind as that shown by the man who tells you he cannot eat bacon or never eats fish, as if it were some peculiar virtue or fineness of quality that inhibited him. " I never take any interest in politics," says one ; " Too busy at the works to want to spend my evenings sitting with a lot of fools on a committee of the council," says another ; yet these are the respectable people, fathers of families, who regard themselves as the backbone of the nation, and they are the men who are most apt to complain if anything goes wrong with the services that they use. " It's too bad," they say, " look at the state of the roads, I don't know why we have a town council, I'm sure I pay enough in rates," or " I was late at work this morning, those rotten trams of ours broke down again." These are the men who take no trouble about public affairs, very likely they don't even trouble to vote or know who their representative is, and they are surprised and complain when they get the sort of government they deserve. They were astonished and dazed at the catastrophe that suddenly broke up their decent ordered existence when the European war broke out, not realising that it was due to the bad citizenship of themselves and others like them in foreign countries. To the Athenian public work was as important as, if not more important than, his private business, and it is this attitude of mind that we wish to recreate. To-day men who are reasonably honest in private life will think nothing of cheating the state or the municipality, not realizing that they are cheating themselves. In some towns even to-day there is a strong civic pride, as in Birmingham, an inheritance of Joseph Chamberlain's reforming zeal in the seventies—but it needs directing, and many things of which we are proud should cause us shame. The stretch of No Man's Land by the Ypres salient is an abomination to the sight, "mere earth desperate and done with," but there are stretches of this country that are quite as hideous and befouled—South Staffordshire and South Lancashire for instance—and they strike more horror into the mind from the fact that they are instances of man's constructive not destructive powers, and that there are still people who are proud of them. The re-creation of the city and of the countryside, so that those who live there can take pleasure and pride in them, is the greatest task of reconstruction that is before us to-day, and it is only by the appearance of a higher ideal in local public life that we shall get more control by the citizens over the affairs of the nation and the Empire. In municipal affairs the citizen has the knowledge ready to his hand, he is himself affected by the action of his local governing authority, the conditions of his locality are those he must himself endure, and he must know what is wrong. If a man lives in Widnes or Bermondsey, he may get used to the smells of chemicals or tanneries but he can hardly like them, and on a return from a holiday it must strike him that the conditions under which he lives call at least for enquiry. It is very easy to get used to ugly conditions, but every successful effort at making a town a worthy place of habitation will have its effect on the neighbouring districts by calling attention to their own defects. Let us consider some of the ways in which the spirit of social service can be utilised in the improvement of central and local government, and see what opportunities there are for the public spirited.

THE VOLUNTARY WORKER AND THE ORGANISED COMMUNITY

During the last few years the great increase in the activities of the State and the municipality, and their incursion into the social life of the people, has offered extended opportunities for those who wish to utilise their spare time in the service of the community. At one time it appeared as if the old conception of the efforts of the residents of a locality being utilised to carry out the common work of the district was going to be replaced by the paid official, their participation being restricted to the few who served on elective bodies such as the School Board, Town Council and Board of Guardians, but although the number of officials has increased and is increasing, yet at the same time the sphere of the voluntary worker has expanded. As the work formerly done by individuals or societies has been taken over by public authorities and extended and co-ordinated, so it has been found necessary to associate with the paid official the voluntary worker, who can bring to bear a detailed knowledge of a district and introduce a personal touch into the work, and apply general provisions to particular instances.

This has been specially exemplified in the sphere of elementary education. In schools provided by public authorities and religious bodies alike there had long been bodies known as school managers, whose duty it was to consider the particular needs of the school educationally, to appoint teachers, make representations as to structural alterations, or special provisions for different sorts of work. In poor districts these managers, who were generally appointed from social workers and clergy in the district for groups of schools, found it necessary to form sub-committees for dealing with the physical needs of the children, and in some cases to arrange for food and clothing. With the advent of the feeding of school children out of the rates, and the provision of medical inspection and treatment, the duties cast upon the voluntary workers in the schools became more important, and in the large towns especially, and in London in particular, a regular system of children's care committees was set up. In some districts the work of children's care is done by the education committee, but in the case of large towns and of the metropolis this is impossible, owing to the size of the area and the number of schools and children. Hence the falling back upon non-elected voluntary workers.

The provision of meals for school children was long left in the hands of the charitable; in London such societies as the Destitute Children's Dinner Society, the Ragged School Union and the Referee Fund led the way, and about 1884 there was a great increase of voluntary feeding all over the country; later, attempts were made to organise these various agencies, a matter of some difficulty owing to the controversy between the advocates of payment by the parents, and those who wished meals provided free, while yet others would have preferred to leave the matter in the hands of the Guardians.

After much controversy the Education Provision of Meals Act was passed whereby the local education authority was empowered to spend money out of the rates in providing free meals for the necessitous. The direct result of this was the formation in London of the School Care Committee and of similar bodies in the country which have now come to form central organising points around which all social work affecting children of school age tends to be grouped. The aim of each committee is to get together a body of voluntary workers who are interested in the children attending the school, such as the clergy of various denominations and their church-workers, managers of boys' clubs and scout leaders, representatives of the various specialised societies such as the Invalid Children's Aid Association and the general charitable organisations of the district. In some cases too, working men and women serve on the committees.

These committees have most important functions; it is their duty to decide what children are necessitous, and give or withhold meals: members attend the medical inspection and follow up the cases, arranging for treatment and endeavouring to persuade parents, where necessary, to take their children to hospitals or clinics for treatment, to consent to operations, pay part of the cost of instruments or spectacles, and generally to follow out the doctor's advice.

Under the Choice of Employment Act and the Labour Exchanges Act it became the duty of the members to advise the children leaving school to attend the Labour Exchange, and to follow up the children who have left so that they shall not be left without guidance. The easiest way is to get children to join clubs, etc., hence the club workers in the neighbourhood are brought into direct contact with the school care committee; sometimes the committee arranges for clubs or old scholars' guilds to be carried on at the school premises.

It will be seen from this very brief reference to the activities of the care committee how much work is involved. The greater part of this is voluntary:

paid organisers may be appointed who will perhaps do part of the inquiry work involved, and much information may be obtained through the school attendance officer, while of course the closest co-operation with the teachers is essential ; but the amount of clerical work involved in a poor school on the part of the secretary requires some one prepared to devote the whole or the greater part of his or her time to the work, while for others visiting and reporting on the homes from which the children come, attending at the school interviewing parents and children, and arranging with teachers, or with organisations outside the innumerable details of small services to individual children, require a high degree of social service, a considerable sacrifice of leisure and much acquaintance with the district worked in and with the technique of investigation. Thus it may be said that the whole work of caring for the physical and recreational needs of school-children depends to-day on an adequate supply of voluntary workers.

It is not always easy to keep up this supply ; there are generally in each district a certain number of social workers, but these have their special interests, and the work of the school care committee requires that a certain number of persons should make it their main work. It is in my opinion very desirable that as many people as possible drawn from the classes whose children attend the elementary school should take part in the work, for only by the active association of the parents can the utmost be got out of the schools and a healthy interest in education aroused. Attempts are made to-day by care committees to arouse this interest by meetings of parents held in the school ; but the active association of these in the work itself will be far more fruitful than any lectures. This, I think, is a point to be borne in mind: I remember not many years ago an educational council being formed for a district, and thereon were placed representatives of everybody who was likely to take an interest in education, clergy settlement workers, club managers, and teachers and representatives of local authorities, with the surprising omission that in an almost entirely working class district no representative of the parents or of the working class was invited to serve. The natural result was that the council was still-born.

Among other agencies that centre round the school care committee may be mentioned the children's country holiday fund, one of the most valuable of all. The object is, by supplementing parents' own payments, to assist town children to go away to the country where they are boarded out in selected homes. In the work of arranging for the homes, collecting subscriptions, supervising the departure and return of the children, a large number of voluntary workers are needed every summer; the work is very pleasant, as the sight of the returning children is a speedy reward for the trouble of the work, and as it does not need so much experience as the various forms of relief, it can be recommended to those who are making a first essay at social service.

The form of social effort outlined above is perhaps more suitable to women than to men, for their experience as to the needs of the children is necessarily greater; but there is need for voluntary work that can be best done by men in the advisory committees of the labour exchanges. The juvenile advisory committees of the labour exchanges are examples of the collaboration of the voluntary worker with a State Department. The evil of blind-alley occupations for boys and girls is now well understood, though that does not mean that they have been remedied. A real endeavour is now made to find out for what trade or occupation each child is most suited when it leaves school, and committees formed of those acquainted with children as well as of those with a knowledge of industry have been set up.

In a small or medium sized town, with a staple trade or trades, the difficulty is not very great, and it is easier to interest employers in the matter owing to the greater local patriotism in the smaller towns, and their natural interest in the labour force on which they will themselves be drawing ; but in London and the larger towns it is harder to get the employers to give time to serve on these committees, as they are probably living some distance from their works, and recruit their labour from wide areas. Yet it is just at this work that the employer can find a useful outlet for his instincts of social service. He has the knowledge of his trade, or possibly of groups of trades, and the advantage to him of serving on these committees will not be restricted to the good done in placing square pegs into square holes, but will also make him aware in a more real and lively manner than before of the workers' side of the question. Writers are wont to deplore the growing separation between master and man, and the lack of the personal touch ; here then is a chance to do something to restore it, and if trade union representatives are also on the committee, another stratum of experience is combined, and the more workmen and employers sit together on committees where the matters under discussion are points of agreement and not of disagreement, the better for the widening of the outlook of each. The J.A.C. provides a meeting ground for employers and employed to look at the industries of the country in a detached manner as partners in the prosperity of the country, and as their immediate aim is the same —that of doing their best for the boys who are the future citizens—there is a chance that they may go further, and consider industries themselves from the point of public services rather than private profit. A similar function may be performed by masters and men sitting on committees dealing with the technical education of young people where again the questions that divide are in abeyance.

Yet another service that has grown rapidly of late years calls for voluntary effort, and that is the various provisions made for birth and infancy: health visiting and assistance at baby clinics or creches, or infant welfare centres, demand a body of workers, and here the married woman's experience can be utilised. Here as elsewhere there is much need for volunteers, although there must necessarily be paid officials, doctors, midwives, etc. The numerous charitable agencies that have long been working in this field are now coming to be grouped together under the health activities of the local authorities; the old fashioned mothers' meeting, which was often regarded rather suspiciously owing to its connection with religious propaganda on the one side and the suspicion of charity on the other, is giving way to the meetings where the doctor and the nurse are the central figures and where everything is done that can stimulate interest in the care of the infants. The infant welfare centre is becoming a means of education for married women, and a focus of thought on all that concerns the home and the infant, and the voluntary worker can do much, apart from the practical work with the infants, in taking part in and inaugurating discussions, a very necessary piece of social work, for now that women have the vote it is necessary that they should learn the bearing of public questions, particularly on the subjects that most concern them, and of all women voters those who most need instruction in the duties and rights of the citizen are the married women in the poorer districts of the great towns.

Here then are some of the ways in which the volunteer can work inside the machine of the local and national administration, but this description is far from being exhaustive ; war-time experiments such as consumers' councils, and more permanent organisations such as committees on soldiers' and sailors' pensions, and for the aged under the Old Age Pensions Act, all provide great scope for persons of every class to give their voluntary services.

We may pause at this point and consider why it is necessary to reinforce the paid official with the voluntary worker. The first reason is the need for local knowledge of conditions : this the paid official can obtain only after some time, and even then he or she is unlikely to have such a close knowledge of a district as those who actually live and work there ; it is undesirable to try to enforce a rigid system over the whole country, for methods suitable to a country district will not do in towns. The habits of life in London, Lancashire or Yorkshire will differ from those in the Midlands or South Wales. In all social advances it is desirable to work with the least possible amount of friction, and the collaboration of people of the neighbourhood, particularly of people whom the new form of social organisation is designed to benefit, will prevent any attempt at rigid uniformity and will have regard to local circumstances and, it may be, prejudices.

Secondly: the paid official is generally very busy, and is frequently almost overwhelmed with office work so as to be unable to undertake the necessary amount of detailed dealings with individuals. Much of the work deals with the least educated portion of the community, much time is taken up listening to long and involved explanations, and in patient explanation—a work best left to voluntary workers.

Thirdly: there is a tendency for officials to become bureaucratic and tied up with red-tape. An important part of the work of the volunteer is the seeking out of the new methods and the making of experiments; for this private money and private work are necessary. As the authors of the Minority Report of the Poor Law put it: "There are many forms of institutional treatment which the various public authorities are not likely themselves to initiate and there are others that they are almost debarred from conducting. There is room for pioneer experiments in dealing with every type of distressed person. . . . In the field of initiating and developing new institutional treatment, whether it be the provision of perfect alms-houses for the aged or the establishment of vacation schools or open-air schools for the children: whether it be the enveloping of the morally infirm or those who have fallen in a regenerating atmosphere of religion and love, or some subtle combination of physical regimen and mental stimulus for the 'town bred hooligan,' very large sums of money can be advantageously used, and are in fact urgently needed."

Fourthly: the services of the local authorities are becoming, each in its own sphere, the natural focus for social service; charity organisation has been tried and has failed, its place has been taken by the extension of the work of the organised community to those spheres of activity formerly left to charity. In the future it is desirable that individual and communal effort should be closely linked up, and this is best done by getting all those who are willing to give their services into touch with the official organisation.

Fifthly: there is the educative influence of the meeting of persons drawn from different classes, occupations, and creeds on a common basis. In towns the old quarrels and competitions of the conflicting religious sects have been much mitigated by the co-operation of their representatives in social work. The working-man or woman serving alongside the middle-class social worker appreciates better his point of view and gains in knowledge, and this tends to check the occasional tendency to undue leniency and over-generosity, while the middle-class worker learns to avoid the pitfall of being unco' guid.

Finally: there is the importance of getting the workers themselves to carry on the work that after all most concerns them. This point is often neglected, but is to my mind vital, the old objection to State and municipal action that it pauperises people to have things done for them, loses its sting when those very people are concerned in the administration of the communal provision of necessary services, or the relief of those in distress.

A word must here be said as to the demarcation of work between the voluntary and the paid worker. It is, I think, clear that the specialist should be a paid official, the nurse, the doctor, the teacher and the midwife are all professional people, and are entitled to be paid for their services, and to have their hours of work and hours of leisure clearly laid down. This has not always been done in the past, nor is it always done at the present; charitable people frequently seem to think that because the element of social service bulks so large in these professions that extra work should be done by them for nothing or extra hours worked. Well-intentioned persons will start a baby clinic and expect the doctor to give his services as an act of charity in the same way as others will expect public entertainers, actors, actresses and musicians to give performances free for charity. Local authorities sometimes fall into the same error. When school meals were started it was suggested that the teachers should supervise them in their meal times, forgetting that the wearing nature of the work of the elementary school teacher made a good rest in the middle of the day a necessity; or again, a treat will be provided for school children on a Saturday, and it will be calmly assumed that the teachers should give up their holiday without pay "for the sake of the little ones." It would be just as reasonable to expect the railway to carry them for nothing or the caterer to provide a free meal. I mention the case of the teacher particularly because no class of worker, except perhaps the public entertainer, is so much exposed to this form of imposition. I repeat it is fundamentally unfair, and a form of sweating. The work of organisation and the bulk of the office work should, I hold, be done by paid workers, though very often it is not ; here again some local authorities are among the worst offenders. A municipality ought not to expect to have its clerical work done for nothing, the work of the secretary of a care committee of a school or schools in a poor London district is a full time job and should be paid for as such, the work of the volunteer is supplementary. The volunteer supplies the personal touch, visiting and investigation, making decisions in individual cases, initiating new experiments, and thinking out extensions of the work, and co-operating with other agencies fall within his sphere, but the less time spent on mere office work the better.

THE SOCIAL SERVICE OF THE PAID OFFICIAL

There is a widespread distrust of officials as a class, and of "officialism" as a system. Members of Parliament and newspapers are fond of denouncing the horde of officials, or the stupidities of the official mind, and the ramifications of red-tape, so that there is a tendency to ignore the enormous amount of valuable work done by the much abused official, and the great devotion and energy that he brings, as a rule, to his work.

The current conception of the official as a man or woman who stays in an office all day going through files and minuting correspondence is too narrow to-day: it belongs to the past rather than to the present or the future. Let us grant the drawbacks of the official, the red-tape, the circumscribed outlook, the timidity and narrow-mindedness that are usually alleged and examine the service of the State and the municipality as a sphere for the exercise of active social service. This criticism is, I think, becoming less true than formerly.

The idea of the State or municipal service being rather a dull but safe job for anyone to undertake, a play for safety as it were in the game of life, though still extant, is giving way to a sense of the importance of the social service rendered and a realisation of the possibilities of adventure in breaking new ground that is offered to the civil servant. The State and the municipality more than ever before are concerned with the lives of the citizens in their every aspect, especially social and industrial. It is true that the civil service does not offer great pecuniary rewards nor high honours except to the few, but it offers power, responsibility, and social service.

There have been in the past great civil servants, such as Chadwick or Sir J. Simon, whose work has profoundly affected the social life of the nation, although at the time in which they lived the dominant idea of individualism and *laissez faire* greatly restricted their powers of usefulness. To-day, especially during and after the war, there has been a great extension of State control, and government is probably more sensitive to the ideas of the general public than ever before. Take for instance the work of an official in the Ministry of Labour, he must know much beyond the routine of his office: he must know what are the ideas behind this or that symptom of labour unrest. He must know something of the psychology of masters and men: in a word, to fit himself for his task he must know people, not only things. This means that he must have the widest possible outlook. If he has only "the official mind" he will be a failure.

During the late war numbers of men in the army

did a good deal more than their bit owing to the powerful feeling set up by the motives from which they entered the service, and in a good battalion there was a keenness in all ranks to make the section, platoon, company, or battalion the best ; it is necessary to transmute this feeling of the duty of military service into social service. If every director of education gets the same spirit into the teachers of his locality as the good C.O. got into his battalion, and every head teacher regards himself as a company commander in the war against ignorance, great advances might be made, and this same spirit should extend to the staff although they may be engaged on dull routine clerical work, whether in a government department, or in the office of a local authority.

Take again the education service of this country. An enormous responsibility rests on those who have so large a share in forming the mind of the next generation, and everything depends on the spirit in which this work is carried on. If it is regarded merely as a means of getting a living, and mentally compared with the work of the clerk or the factory worker, it will be a failure ; the teacher must regard himself rather as an artist dealing with a most plastic material, and must have a high ideal of what is the kind of citizen that he wishes his pupils to become. The profession of teaching is little appreciated in this country, and therefore the salaries tend to be very low. This is the root of the matter, people are willing to pay for what they appreciate, and a comparison of the salaries paid to various classes of workers will show where in the scale the teacher comes as compared, let us say, with the professional athlete or the popular entertainer. The first requirement of the teacher is that he shall be an enthusiast for education, but it can hardly be said that in our schools to-day we have a very high standard of enthusiasm. In our secondary schools the profession of teaching is frequently adopted by men who are not specially interested, but are fond of games, appreciate the fairly lengthy holidays and the conditions of life, and cannot think of anything else to do, while the elementary teacher has often been attracted to the profession by the desire of gaining a slightly higher position in the social scale. It should be our aim to attract to the education service the best minds in the country, and to do that the service should be made attractive. It is impossible for men and women to devote themselves to teaching if they are continually worried about the difficulty of making ends meet. Despite admitted evils and many shortcomings, there is a vast amount of good social work done by teachers, both inside and outside school. Many devote not a little of their scanty means and leisure to work with and for the children who are in their charge, and where encouragement is given by the local authorities much useful experimental work can be done. Teachers have arranged for school journeys, whereby town children are taken into the country and learn to know something of the history of the district visited, and can see something of nature that will assist them to appreciate the book work when they return to town. Other teachers will experiment with open air classes or new methods, but all these require the backing of those who have the power in educational matters. A position of great authority and opportunity for school service is that of director of education to some large education authority. If he is a man of vision and can influence his council he can do most valuable work in getting beyond mere routine, and in adapting the education, elementary or other, to the needs of the locality.

Again the reports of the medical officer of the Board of Education show the varied and interesting experiments undertaken by the school doctor, and the public medical service that is now being co-ordinated under the Ministry of Health, gives scope enough for anyone. Medical officers of health set a high standard of service as a rule and regard their work as part of the world-wide crusade against disease. Much can be done by paid officials of local governing bodies to assist in building up a healthy local patriotism; councillors may come and go, but he remains, and is bound to exercise a great influence.

I would emphasise the importance of getting the social service outlook as widely diffused as possible among those employed by the central local governing bodies of the country. There is such a thing as the Government stroke and ca' canny is not unknown among Government officials. In the service of the State the incentive of private profit is lacking, and the fear of losing the job is not so great as in private employment, but this is or should be compensated by the absence of the feeling that vitiates so many of the arguments addressed to the workers in privately controlled undertakings to increase their efforts, that they are only working to pile up a fortune for some individual or individuals. There is, on the other hand, the danger of the slackness of the ordinary sensual man, and the tyranny of habit and routine. For some reason, in this country while we are always ready to credit our civil servants who work in India, Egypt or any other of our various dependencies with the highest sense of duty and public spirit, we are apt to depreciate and run down the men and women of the home civil service and the municipal official. As a man once said in moving a vote of thanks to a temporary Government officer, "Officials generally get more kicks than halfpence." A continual stream of depreciation, seldom varied by praise for good work done, is poured out on the civil service: this is not only unfair but stupid, for appreciation makes good work. It is unfortunate that Ministers of State are seldom justified by their achievements as heads of their departments by the general public: if they were, it would be worth their while to take more pains to get a spirit of keenness and contentment among their subordinates. An added reason for the acceptance of this point of view is the probability of large extensions of public control in the near future. The difficulties that face us to-day are not so much the concrete difficulties of organisation as the abstract one of psychology. Wide proposals are being canvassed for the extension of the sphere of the State into the realms of transport, and even coal production: no one doubts that the organisation of the railways for instance is possible as a practical proposition, the doubt is of the spirit in which the system will be worked. A motive instead of self-interest must be found, and that motive must be that which actuates the social worker and the best civil servants, and which so powerfully operated during the war, that of the service of the community.

SERVICE ON A LOCAL COUNCIL

The system of local government in this country, whereby the paid official is subordinated to councils of elected persons who not only make rules and regulations for the governance of the city, the county or the district, but actually administer them at the same time, throws a big responsibility on the ordinary citizen, but offers him a great opportunity for fruitful social service.

On the County or Town Council, or on the Board of Guardians, the citizen can find an enormous opportunity for serving his fellows, and a practical training in the art of government. Local public life is a training ground for the citizen wherein he may appreciate the difficulties of government, and where he may learn how the country is governed and what are the limitations of governing bodies, and may be trained to take his part in national and even international affairs.

It is customary to sneer at the politics of the parish pump and to talk of local Bumbles, but few stop to consider alternatives, or to weigh the amount of good done with the occasional stupidities.

The number of men and women in this country giving unpaid services on local bodies runs into thousands, and the wonder is not that there are failures, but that on the whole there is success. There are always a certain number who seek office for the pride of calling themselves Councillor or Alderman and a few who have axes to grind and who get on to governing bodies to further their own interests, or to prevent the remedying of abuses, but the great majority must be credited with a genuine civic sense and a desire to work for the best interests of the neighbourhood.

The Board of Guardians is an obvious instance of the need for the disinterested citizen who is prepared to give time to the arduous and not always pleasant work. This body is most often considered as the classic ground of Bumbledom, and the very name of the Poor Law suggests Oliver Twist. Certainly there have been great abuses in the past. The opportunities for petty dishonesty or even considerable corruption in the matter of contracts are greater than in any other body. There have been scandals in the past, and suspicions of Tammany methods in relief that are likely to be justified here and there, where the power of giving sums of money to individuals has been entrusted to interested persons with a low sense of civic responsibility. It is all the more necessary to call attention to the great volume of devoted work done by Guardians all over the country. Meetings of the board and its committees, visits to institutions and schools consume a lot of time, and the work is not easy—no system of relief is—and the system of English Poor Law has been condemned in the well known Majority and Minority Reports, but despite the evils of the system, it is impossible to deny that good work has been done. Some of the Poor Law homes and schools set a very high standard and some infirmaries can rank as good hospitals. The Board of Guardians is now under sentence of death, and its functions are to be distributed among other authorities, but the work will have to be done just the same. There are in this country many men and women who have devoted their lives to the detailed work of the Poor Law who have acquired great knowledge, and who do their work in the best spirit of service. Their devotion must not be ignored, particularly that of the women members. Women have served on boards of guardians for many years, but are only gradually finding their way on to other municipal bodies, yet their presence is essential. In any matters concerning women, and children, or institutions, women have far more knowledge than men. Faults in the domestic arrangement of a workhouse or home are seen at once by them, and there are few more ludicrous sights than a committee of men trying to settle questions such as what kind of clothes shall be purchased for the children, or how many cleaners or cooks are required.

More important to-day is the work of county, town and district councils. In country districts county business is still rather an affair for the local gentry, and it is sometimes suggested that the rural parts of the country are still dominated by the aristocracy. Whether it is true is another matter, but if it is, it speaks well for the public spirit of those who do the work. It is one of the traditions of English life that wealth has its duties, and whatever may be the case with the *nouveaux riches* the tradition is still held by many of those who have been for some time settled in a country that they owe the country public service. The great unpaid magistracy is often sneered at, and doubtless there are those who are magistrates only because thay desire to put J.P. after their names, but the fact remains that a big amount of work is performed by the local magistrates which is on the whole fairly satisfactory, while county council business means extra work to the busy man, and demands some attention from the idle. The urban municipalities are called on to perform a great variety of functions and practically any form of social work can be found among their undertakings. The keen educationalist can here endeavour to get his theory put in practice and those who are interested in children can find plenty to do in the education and health committee. Those who are interested in athletics can see that the parks are utilised and open spaces obtained where possible. Housing is a favourite subject with many, and the working out of a scheme for municipal houses, finding out the best plans, etc., will be not only useful work but agreeable. Very many people are engaged in work of an abstract nature and lose the pleasure of getting concrete things done: if the enthusiast does not allow his energy to outrun his financial discretion he can get all the pleasure a man finds in having a house built by interesting himself in the council's schemes.

Many people are deterred from social work by a feeling that they are not suited for it, perhaps they do not get on with children, dislike to see the sick, or are too shy to visit and talk with people of a different class: on the council every quality can be utilised, the business man can find an opening for his experience on the tramways, gas or electricity works or finance committees, the architect on the housing and town planning committee, and the doctor can interest himself on the public health and asylums, the engineer will constantly be consulted on technical points arising from the equipment of the various undertakings and institutions. One person might devote himself especially to the public library and see to it that the books provided were those most suitable to those who frequent it—the musician can try to improve the position of music in the parks. Artists are not often found on public bodies, but surely here is their chance, the great works of art of the past were produced mostly for the community. The city should be an expression of the mind of the people who live there, let us hope that most of our cities are not. To-day efforts are being made to organise our city life on a more conscious plan—it is realised that our cities are mere ugly collections of factories and dwellings and frequently our public buildings are little better. Compare the average Town Hall with some of the Guild Halls that survive from the past—few are worthy to stand by them. Here and there, as for instance at Coventry or Oxford, one finds a fine Town Hall, but in general there is very little of which to boast. If those who care for art would endeavour to influence municipal bodies in the right direction they would do more good than can be done by societies for the protection of ancient buildings, and other outside organisations.

As Mr. W. R. Lethaby says, " If ever we are to have a time of architecture again it must be founded on a love for the city, a worship of home and nation. No planting down a few costly buildings, ruling some straight streets, provision of fountains, or setting up of a number of stone or bronze dolls, is enough without the enthusiasm for corporate life and common ceremonial. Every noble city has been a crystallisation of the contentment, pride and order of the community. A period of architecture is a flowing tide. If the municipalities would spend less on 'art' and more on acquiring fine quality in all ordinary forms of workmanship, the situation would soon be improved. Cleaner streets and tidier railway stations would be better than all the knowledge of all the styles. An endeavour to better the city in introducing civic patriotism would be sure in due time to bring a fit method of expression. When we see how prompt is an idea—the cause, order, form—to boys, it does seem possible that men too may organise themselves into lovers of the city, seekers after discipline."

It is not merely for the sake of the work that can be done on the council that I lay stress on the municipalities, it is an example of citizenship. We have said that this training is valuable for those who wish to take part in public life on a wider stage, it is more than that, it is essential. No democracy can be carried on successfully without the fullest possible knowledge of how and why things are done: ignorance breeds suspicion, and one of the best ways of gaining knowledge in the sphere of government is to govern. A healthy active local life is necessary for a healthy democratic central government, and an active municipality, where local questions are really discussed, and where local elections are fought on matters of principle rather than on the rival popularity of the publican and the baker, educates not only the elected but the electors.

An extremist friend of mine was elected to a local council, and after a few weeks a friend of his of like views said to him, "We don't seem to have heard much of you since you got on the council." "What do you mean?" said the other—"Well you haven't been thrown out yet," replied his friend. "I realised then," he told me, "how much I'd learned since I had been elected, for my view used to be the same as his, 'make a row.'" Therefore one of the greatest services that the social worker can do is by getting elected on to local bodies help to create a healthy civic feeling and a local patriotism. There are many municipalities to-day that take a healthy pride in their civic work: Bradford and Brighton for instance are well known for the work of their education committees, other towns for the good work of their health committees, or trams. When this kind of rivalry is set up other towns will endeavour to compete, thus raising the standard all round.

There are some social workers who hold themselves aloof from civic life, professing to be above the rough and tumble of a local election, and in many places the government of the town is left to a section of the community. The town council should be regarded as an honourable position, and should have representatives of every class, and the assumption that things would be better done if left to a nominated committee of social workers is short-sighted as well as snobbish. A question of some urgency to the social worker is the increased amount of time necessary to fulfil the duties of a citizen. The London County Council work takes up practically a man's whole time, while in the country county councils are generally filled with the leisured class because no one else can afford to serve. It has been suggested that the representatives should be paid, but there are considerable objections to this. As things are, the paid county councillor would be making a big sacrifice by giving up his ordinary occupation for the hazardous work of sitting on a council, and the fact of his position being also his livelihood would tend to make him unduly subservient to his electors, or perhaps a section of them, and would turn an elective position into a freehold owing to the natural dislike everyone has of doing a man out of his job. Whether a further division of municipalities by areas or functions is possible is not for us to discuss here but it is well to note the danger of paid representatives. To the social worker, at all events, the difficulty is an incentive to work for an increased civic spirit, so that it may be realised by all that work done on local bodies is not time lost, and that employers particularly may consider that the election to a local body of one of their employees is an honour to the firm, and may make up for the time lost to them.

Of late years a number of posts have been created that have a direct connection with social work. These are not filled as a rule by the ordinary methods of examination, but by persons selected for their experience and knowledge of social matters. These offer a career for those who though keen on social work cannot afford to devote all their time without remuneration. The pay is not as a rule high and the hours are sometimes long, but there is considerable scope for the enthusiast, and as the higher posts in the civil service are now being increasingly thrown open to women there is the chance of reaching positions of influence. During the war women have successfully invaded many departments formerly staffed entirely by men and have proved their worth.

The following are some of the posts open to women experienced in social work.

Sanitary Inspectors.
Factory Inspectors.
Inspectors under the Midwives Act.
Infant Life Protection Inspectors.
Poor Law Inspectors.
Education Inspectors.
Health Visitors.

National Insurance Inspectors.
Organisers of Care Committees (London).
Secretaries under the Labour Exchanges Act for Juvenile Advisory Committees.
Managers of Labour Exchanges (Women's side).
Secretaries under the Choice of Employment Act.
Probation Officers.
Housing Inspectors.
Relieving Officers.

CHAPTER V

THE QUALIFICATIONS AND TRAINING OF THE SOCIAL WORKER

THE first qualification for any one who wishes to engage in social work is sympathy. The social worker is coming, as a rule, from a class that has many advantages of wealth, leisure and education, and is endeavouring to share those advantages with others who are less well circumstanced and whose surroundings and opportunities are wholly different.

Success or failure will depend in the main on the attitude he or she adopts towards those whom it is desired to assist, and the extent to which the social worker can put himself mentally into the position of other people. Men and women of the upper and middle classes have certain conventions and a certain mental outlook that are altogether different from those of the working-class people ; they have their standards by which they value those with whom they come in contact, and certain virtues which they prize ; but it must be remembered that working people have their own standards, different but not necessarily wrong.

We all have our pet virtues and vices, and as a rule the virtues that are approved and the vices that are deplored by any class are those which appear most conducive or noxious to the interests of that class. To take an instance; middle-class people are apt to lay great stress on the virtue of thrift, and many a sermon, lay and clerical, has been preached to working folk on this theme; indeed there has been a tendency among some social workers to elevate this somewhat unlovely habit to the highest place of all. This is perfectly natural.

The normal middle-class citizen has a surplus over his expenditure on necessaries and puts by for a rainy day. Why should not others do the same instead of being so extravagant and shiftless? Surely it is desirable that the poor should save and not come on the rates or call upon the charitable for assistance. This attitude is due to a natural desire for self-protection. Now, from the worker's point of view this appears as a design to keep the poor in their place, content with low wages, so that they shall not demand a larger share of the good things of life from the rich; further, in everyday life thrift is not a virtue that is admired; on the contrary, it is regarded as stinginess, and open-handedness and generosity are the admired virtues. This is easily intelligible from the position of the mass of the workers who can never be sure that they may not themselves be needing assistance very soon, and so we are struck by the amazing charity of the poor to the poor, the readiness with which one poor household will take into their home and support a friend who is out of a job, and the ready response to whip round for a widow left penniless, or for similar cases of misfortune. Hence, too, the difficulty of maintaining a benefit society on sound financial lines, owing to the readiness of the members to give in cases of hardship. I have been present at a meeting of a trade union branch where three cases were brought up in one evening, where, although the member had no claim on the funds, yet in each case the members voted to break the rules rather than see their comrade suffer. Solidarity is the only weapon of the poor, and no preaching of the gospel according to Samuel Smiles will have any effect under present conditions.

Again, a very poor family will spend all the money derived from an insurance policy on an expensive funeral. The social worker is apt to be irritated, thinking of the comforts that might have been bought with it, forgetting that perhaps that very day she has been urging self-respect and proper pride, and that, wasteful though this expense may be, it is in reality only a means of expression of proper pride, the tradition of the neighbourhood being that a deceased relative should be put away with all possible circumstance. A poor funeral will have a similar effect on the social standing of the family as a failure to appear in evening dress at some function would have on the middle-class person, and until the social worker is prepared to cut off all his or her expenditure which is due simply to social habit, it is illogical to expect it of others.

These are only instances to illustrate the first thing that the would-be social worker must learn, that is, a thorough appreciation of the outlook of those with whom he will come in contact.

It is no good merely noting these views and putting them down to prejudice or ignorance ; there is always a reason. For instance, the objection on the part of many working-class parents to letting their girls go to domestic service seems incomprehensible to many, though a little inquiry will show that there are reasons which, though not absolute, are entitled to consideration.

The distaste for breaking up the family and sending children to live away from home is very much greater among working-class people than among those who are accustomed to send their children to boarding-schools at a tender age, and the lot of the domestic in a situation where only one is kept, or perhaps in a lodging-house, is not always to be judged by the experience of those who come from well-to-do homes where the mistress takes care of her maids and gives good conditions. And the loss to the family exchequer entailed by one member leaving the home to live out is a contributory factor.

A further point calling for sympathetic understanding is in the matter of manners. Sometimes the poor are accused of bad manners, but the accusation might be equally well made—and sometimes is—against certain social workers. The middle-class person is likely to commit as many solecisms through ignorance of the conventions obtaining down east as would the worker visiting in Mayfair. An example or two will make this clear: in many working-class circles it is not the custom to carry on conversation at meals, and unless this is understood you may feel awkward, and think that your hosts or guests are shy, or annoyed, or desire you to go. Again, a boy may come to tea with you, and keep on sitting there afterwards while you wonder how to get him to go. In your own class it would not be polite to tell him it was time to depart, but he will expect it, and would think it rudeness to go away before you had suggested it.

To sympathise one must understand, and to understand one must know; and that is what the social worker has got to try and do: he must rid himself of the idea that he is a superior person with a superior "kultur" who is coming down at considerable personal inconvenience to teach ignorant persons. He must realise that though superior in some things he is inferior in others, and that he has quite as much to learn as to teach. He must be prepared to suspend judgment until he has attained experience. Too often the poor are weighed in the scales of middle-class virtue and condemned by standards that they do not accept.

The social worker must try to put himself on a level with those among whom he is going to work, realising that they are and must be his fellow-workers in endeavouring to create a better state of affairs.

First impressions take a long time to efface, and it makes a great deal of difference to those who are entering on social work for the first time on what tooting they meet people of another class. We are all apt to judge people of another class by the few instances with which we are brought into contact; the average middle-class woman takes her ideas of the working class from her domestic servants. The average well-to-do person who lives in a village will tell you that the unemployed are wasters and drunkards, arguing from the village ne'er-do-weel, and forgetting that the unemployed man with any "go" in him does not stop in the village. In the same way the average working man will judge employers from the foremen whom he knows, or from a single employer or the landlord. If the social worker's first contact with working people is with those who come to relief centres he will not be favourably impressed.

I am strongly of the opinion that it is a wrong beginning for the young social worker to start with the administration of relief. This puts him or her into a wrong position from the start. No one is at his ease when asking alms, and the position of donor and recipient is one of the hardest in which to maintain friendship. It is never easy to be perfectly friendly and natural with a man when you are trying to get him to lend you a fiver.

The difficulty of the position is exactly hit off in the poem by Mary Coleridge on "An Insincere Wish Addressed to a Beggar."

> We are not near enough to love,
> I can but pity all your woe;
> For wealth has lifted me above,
> And falsehood set you down below.
>
> If you were true we still might be
> Brothers in something more than name;
> And were I poor, your love to me
> Would make our differing bonds the same.
>
> But golden gates between us stretch,
> Truth opens her forbidding eyes;
> You can't forget that I am rich,
> Nor I that you are telling lies.
>
> Love never comes but at Love's call
> And pity asks for him in vain;
> Because I cannot give you all,
> You give me nothing back again.
>
> And you are right with all your wrong,
> For less than all is nothing too;
> May Heaven beggar me ere long,
> And truth reveal herself to you.

To plunge straight into relief work then, means that you will get your first impression of working people as a set of folk out for what they can get; the best run relief society will tend to attract towards it a large number of cadgers, and even as a worker at a school care committee, in the sample of society with which you will be brought into contact, there will be a larger proportion of failures, weaklings, and shiftless persons than the normal, so that you will get a distorted view of conditions and be hard put to it to steer between the pitfalls of over sentimentality and self-righteousness. I have known a young girl starting work set to visiting distress committee cases where the families had pawned practically everything and where conditions were at the very worst, with the inevitable result that she became upset and unbalanced.

It is better, I think, for the aspirant to start work where the relationship is easier. Work among boys and girls in clubs or scout troops is perhaps the best way to begin. Children are responsive and hopeful, and the work is interesting. It gives scope for whatever powers one may have, singing, playing, dancing or swimming, boxing or gymnastics. One does not feel such a fool if there is something one can do in this way, and one is very apt to feel a fool when starting social work. Again the consciousness of a common aim, and the fact that the children support the club by payments, give rise to *esprit de corps* and lead to independence, so that a natural relationship is established. Once this is done, knowledge of working-class conditions and outlook will soon be learned from casual conversation, and such knowledge is a valuable check on the information obtained by more inquisitorial means, for as there is no object to be gained the truth comes out.

From time to time I have collected several remarks made by small East London boys which seem to me valuable and worth keeping in mind by social workers.

"A pal is a bloke that knows all about yer, and yet loves yer," was a definition of a friend supplied by a boy: modest but true. It is not much good for the social worker to know all about the conditions of life in the neighbourhood or all about a family unless it leads him to love the people who live there, not as "the poor," but as fellow human beings. His knowledge will be useless without sympathy, and I would say that to know all about people must lead to being fond of them: if not the knowledge is incomplete.

"A gentleman is a bloke that is the same to everybody," was the definition made by one of a number of boys who had been trying to find the right meaning of this rather difficult word. Some suggested he was rich, others that he did no work, but this carried the day. It is of fundamental importance in dealing with those who may regard themselves as your social inferiors to treat them in the same way you would anybody else: some people will tell you that they cannot get on with working people—they don't know what to talk to them about. All they have to do is to behave as they ordinarily would and talk about any topics of general interest. It is quite unnecessary to think that you must talk down to people or they will not understand: the more independence and character the working man or woman has the more will they rightly resent this form of patronage. Be natural.

"Only a working-woman knows what a working-woman has to go through," was the reason given to me by a boy of sixteen for giving votes to women. Social workers are apt not to realise this and to demand an impossibly high standard. Some visitors will call on washing-day and return to a committee and give a bad report on the tidiness and cleanliness of a home:

others will not appreciate the unending struggle against dirt and overwork carried on by the average mother with several small children in a poor district. The wonder is, not that the work is sometimes badly done, but that it is ever done at all. It is a good corrective for the social worker to do his own or her own domestic work for a few months, so as to learn what it is like under comparatively favourable conditions without the worry of making ends meet and no children to look after.

I met a small boy in the street one day and we walked along together. "Where are you off to?" said he. "I'm going home to tea," said I. "Oh, I'm going home to see if there is any tea," was his reply, thus drawing a very useful economic distinction. It is well to keep clearly in mind, if you are one of those to whom meal-times come with almost monotonous regularity, that to others there is the question always present—Where is to-morrow's dinner to come from? During the war this doubt has been present in the minds of a good many of all classes during the shortage of certain necessaries, so that perhaps it does not need so much emphasis as formerly. To the wife of the casual labourer, for instance, there is always the anxiety as to the amount that will be available for the household expenses for the week. If she is not a good manager do not lecture her too severely; it is not easy to manage on a sum varying from two to three pounds to nothing at all. If she adopts an attitude of "sufficient for the day is the evil thereof," can you wonder?

Apropos of a royal visit to East London a very small boy remarked, "Some say as 'ow the King doesn't do no work; he does; but the difference between 'im and us is that 'e can 'ave a relish with 'is tea." It is well to remember that apart from "the relish with your tea" people are very much alike in all classes, and that the same passions and desires that animate you animate them. If a girl you are interested in insists on spending her scanty money on dress fripperies instead of on good, dull, wearing material and fees for evening classes, remember that such predilections are not confined to any one class. This story might also be borne in mind with advantage by some working-men, exponents of the new and inverted snobbery, who think that no one but a manual worker does any work, and remind them that all work does not make corns on the hands.

There is a greater tendency now to get working-men and women to serve on committees that were formerly confined to the middle class, and this serves to prevent the point of view becoming too one-sided. Service on these committees will be a great help to the beginner in realising the worker's point of view.

In all social work there is the great danger that must be avoided of treating people as cases, and grouping them in categories and statistical tables, so that one forgets that all the time one is dealing with individuals. The case-paper system has many advantages, but it rather encourages this mistake by presenting a rather bald *resumé* of facts from which the human characteristics have been extracted. This danger is one to which official bodies and Government departments are prone: it is the function of the volunteer worker to correct it.

For myself, I believe that every endeavour should be made to keep before the minds of social workers, especially when working on committees, the fact that their clients are men and women with the same human relationships as themselves, and the like passions. Never refer to applicants for relief as "the woman" or "the man," rather Mrs. Smith or Mr. Jones, otherwise they become colourless abstractions. One sometimes sees in a case-paper a phrase such as "a relative sometimes assists with money." How dull! Why not "Uncle Joe gives a bit when he's been lucky with the horses," and introduce the human touch. I remember a case being brought up to a committee wherein it was stated that the father of the family was "unsatisfactory," which might mean anything, drink, gambling, laziness or brutality, to the members of the committee, who did not know the case. I happened to have a letter from a small son who was in the country, which ended up with "Give my love to my dear, dear, dear, old dad," which seemed to show that whatever the visitor's opinion of Mr. Barnes might be he was not so unsatisfactory to one who knew him intimately.

There is also no reason and no excuse for failing to treat applicants with courtesy, keeping them waiting in order to show their unimportance, allowing them to stand when a chair could be provided, or entering a house without being invited.

Cheerfulness is a great asset to the social worker: it is no good worrying, and if at times you do get depressed, there is no reason why you should make everybody else miserable as well. I think that people who can't be cheerful had better try some other kind of work. One sometimes meets people who have given up long years to work in some district and are chronically depressed. They take a gloomy view of everything and say that they can see no result of their work, and that the poor are so ungrateful. The results of work are seldom visible to the worker, as changes come about almost imperceptibly and the effects are often indirect. William Morris's words in "The Dream of John Ball" have their application to the efforts of many social workers. "I pondered all these things, and how men fight and lose the battle, and the thing they fought for comes about in spite of their defeat, and when it comes turns out not to be what they meant, and other men have to fight for what they meant under another name."

It is only after some time that one can get the proper perspective and realise what part one's efforts have played towards the solution of any social problem. As to ingratitude, one must remember that whatever may be one's own view there is a profound though unspoken feeling in the minds of the working classes that they have been in some way cheated out of their birthright, and that all that is done for them is only a small instalment of their due—crumbs as it were, from Dives' table—and so that there is no real reason for gratitude, a view with which the present writer has much sympathy.

The next point to emphasise is the importance of seeing things as a whole. Much endeavour has been wasted because people have got down into their own little puddle and look with a jealous eye on intruders, or become so obsessed with the particular evil against which they are delivering a frontal attack that they even oppose the efforts of others who are really turning the flank of the position.

It is of the utmost importance to see things as a whole. Many social workers are like the small boy who, bathing in the sea for the first time and getting a mouthful of salt water, called out, "Hi, Bill, don't come in here, I've struck a bad patch." The patch may be drink, housing, sexual immorality or hooliganism, but it is all part of the sea of poverty.

Another danger somewhat akin to the last is that enthusiasm for an institution or a society may become so great that the means becomes an end; interest in running the society becomes greater than grappling with the evil that it has been formed to overthrow. This danger is common to all institutions, religious, political and social, but is particularly dangerous in the case of social betterment societies created to deal with a specific evil or with poverty in general, where their true aim should be to work for their own elimination. It is almost like the old idea that the poor were created in order to give the rich the opportunity of exercising the virtue of charity. It leads to jealousy of intruders, to rivalry and overlapping, and often to opposition to those who are working for the eradication of the same evil although on different lines; in fact, the society becomes a vested and even an obstructive interest. On the other hand, it is important for all social reformers to keep in touch with some form of practical work which will bring them into contact with the individual. The besetting sin of the scientific type of social reformer is his failure to make allowance for the idiosyncrasies of the individual. Reformers of this sort make plans for rearranging society or some branch of society's work, whereby all the round pegs shall be sorted out and put into round holes, and all the square pegs into square holes, forgetting the infinite number of pegs that are neither round nor square.

They make arrangements for the ordering of others' lives on what seem to them to be ideal principles; but they have themselves got so accustomed to deal with mankind in types and categories that they have over-simplified the problem—their categories are too narrow and they have lost sight of the individual man and woman.

For these the proper medicine is a return to active work among those whom they hope to benefit by their schemes. They have to realise again the sort of material of which they have to make use and the disheartening way things have of turning out otherwise than was intended.

Another type of social reformer or revolutionary idealist, generally drawn from another class, becomes impressed with certain evils, and convinced that only certain fundamental changes will do any good. His ideas become fixed, and he talks of the capitalist class without the least realisation of the individuals who form that somewhat nebulous category. For him the capitalist has ceased to be a human being with feelings and desires like his own ; he is a sort of economic man pursuing with intensity his one aim in life, the exploitation of the worker. This type of man will criticise and condemn all methods of social advance that do not directly square with his formulae, and will repeat his shibboleths without any attempt to work out their practical application. In despair he waits for the social revolution without any real attempt to further it. Here again a dose of practical work is the remedy. The dreamer must keep his feet on the earth and the thinker must come out of his study. Active social work in a small sphere will teach both the lesson they have forgotten, that all social changes ultimately deal with the individual, and that the collection of individuals that compose the nation or any section of it is distinctly intractable material that requires to be well worked upon before it will run into their moulds.

The social worker must endeavour to see things in their right proportion. One of the commonest mistakes is that of judging everybody by the same standard, imagining that something that would be extremely distasteful to oneself is equally so to others. Thus certain forms of work and certain occupations will seem particularly monotonous to those who first come into contact with them, repetition work in factories, or the occupation of a doorkeeper or a lift man. In a tube train you will hear some one say, " Fancy spending all one's time opening and shutting gates and ushering people in and out of trains." As a fact this work is not more monotonous than many other forms ; indeed, to the psychologist it might be absorbingly interesting. The fact is that most of the work that has to be done to-day is on the whole dull, and though this may be a general condemnation of our civilisation, it does not mean that each person is affected in the same way. There are persons who like a routine job where they can let their thoughts stray to other things, and there are people who like heavy and dirty jobs. I knew a lad who found a positive pleasure in coal-heaving.

This is not in any way to subscribe to the complacent doctrine held by some people who are well situated in life that the rich have just as much to bear as the poor, and that the pleasures of the poor are suited to their capacity for enjoyment, but rather to guard against the danger of judging by one's own feelings.

People who come from houses with plenty of servants where the domestic machine runs easily, are apt to be over-impressed by dirt and disorder and exaggerate their effects; while others with cultivated minds will fail to see how people can enjoy the sort of entertainments prevalent in poor districts.

The social reformer must beware of trying to act as God and making man in his own image; we should most of us be very unhappy in each other's paradises; the failure of many well-intentioned schemes has been due to people giving the poor what they thought would be good for them, without studying the psychology of those for whom they were going to cater.

It is hardly necessary to add that the work of social service requires great patience and tolerance, a sense of justice, and an infinite capacity for suffering fools gladly.

Patience, because things move very slowly, and years of effort are needed before any results are obtained worth mentioning, and because you are working with human beings whose minds are not as highly trained as your own. Much time will be consumed in explanations of things which are to you simple, but to those unaccustomed to them, very hard to grasp; tolerance, because you will have to work with many people who do not see things as you do, young people in a hurry and old people who have outgrown their enthusiasms and their capacity for receiving new ideas, and all sorts of cranks who will misunderstand and possibly misrepresent you. There is, too, always a fair proportion of fools, many of them in positions of importance.

TRAINING OF THE SOCIAL WORKER

We may divide the training of the social worker into two branches, practical and theoretical, though the two should go hand-in-hand. The best training for practical work is to assist a more experienced person. The methods of inquiry can be learnt by working with the Charity Organisation Society, a Children's Care Committee, or the Invalid Children's Aid Association. Visiting people in their homes is good experience, and the chief requisites are tact and sympathy; a little general conversation before putting questions will assist in enabling the visitor to get some idea of the kind of person she is visiting and indicating to her the best way of approach. The filling up of case-papers is merely a matter of accuracy, and calls for a realisation of what are the essential points and an appreciation of what is the object of the inquiry. It is a great mistake, in my opinion, to take up an attitude of suspicion; mistrust breeds mistrust, and if you look as if you thought some one was telling lies to you the result will be that lies will be told.

Club work requires firmness and impartiality before everything. Some people are born disciplinarians while others seem to be perfectly incapable of taking hold; boys are easier to manage than girls, as there is more opportunity for working off superfluous energy in games or gymnastics. It is fatal to make favourites or allow yourself to favour a certain clique or a particular individual. It is well for the student to work with a number of different institutions, and if possible in a variety of districts, so as to be able to compare different methods and not draw too wide inferences from one particular district.

After the initial training each student will probably find out what particular line of work attracts him or her most, and which is the most suitable; some will be most interested in children, others in adults, some in health-visiting or welfare work, others in organising women workers. Some are best in dealing with facts, others with persons, while those who are going to make social work their profession will concentrate on the particular branch in which they intend to serve. But it is wise for all to have as wide an experience as possible in order to promote co-operation.

Although it is possible to be too hard and methodical, it is a mistake to ignore the value of business methods in the right place. The social worker should understand the methods of conducting business at committee meetings. Nothing is more common at a meeting of social workers than to find a total absence of business methods. The chairman is often appointed, not from his or her ability in conducting business and keeping members to the point, but from social position, with the result that long rambling discussions take place with no real idea of what is the point at issue. Thus much time is wasted. A good chairman who understands that his job is to get through the agenda, and who can be tactful as well as firm, makes all the difference.

At many meetings the business is left to a few, the chairman and secretary make all the proposals and one or possibly two members say a word now and then, while the rest silently acquiesce. After the meeting they proceed to explain that they were not at all in agreement with this or that proposal, but that they did not like to say anything. This is stupid and unfair, for the object of the meeting is to find out what are the views of the members, who presumably have been selected because they have views, and to obtain a consensus of opinion as to the policy to be adopted. The active spirits will leave the meeting thinking that their proposals have been agreed to and will be carried out, while really the silent majority are lukewarm or hostile.

It is true that committees suffer equally from the over-talkative individual who insists on giving wholly irrelevant details about his work, or on every possible occasion rides his particular hobby instead of dealing with the point at issue, but it is the weakness of the chairman and the slackness of the other members that give the bore his chance. Much time is lost by failure to have a proper agenda and by the unpunctuality of members. This latter may be inevitable occasionally, but is often due to mere carelessness, and the offenders fail to realise that they are not only acting discourteously, but are upsetting the arrangements of the busier members of the committee.

Many social workers wear themselves out through failing to map-out their work ahead ; there is room for scientific management in the use of time, and those who accomplish most are not the people who are always in a hurry. For instance, a few minutes devoted to a study of the map will save much walking about the streets when visiting, and a little consideration of the ordinary habits of a district will prevent many futile visits to people who are out.

THEORETICAL TRAINING

The next requirement is knowledge. The days are, it is to be hoped, past when people without any qualifications other than a good heart and the means of obtaining money plunged straight into social work without any consideration of what was being done by others or what effect their actions were going to have, with the result that they often only increased the evils they tried to prevent.

It is hardly necessary to give instances. The setting up of a night-shelter with cheap meals may only result in attracting all the cadgers to a district already overcrowded: a common lodging-house on model lines may prove to be merely a facility for husbands who wish to desert their families, while profuse gifts to encourage people to go to church may result in the verdict I once heard a boy give in reply to the question "Why are you not a Christian?" "'Cos Christians is all cadgers." And the setting up of an industry for the unemployed with the expenses defrayed by subscriptions, may only lead to an increase of sweating among the regular workers in the trade. The social worker requires training like anybody else, and to the C.O.S. must be given the credit of first seriously taking in hand the education of those associated in its undertakings.

The training required must be practical and theoretical, the practical being obtained by working with more experienced people and the theoretical by reading and courses of lectures. This work the C.O.S. undertook, and they are entitled to all credit as pioneers, for till comparatively recently their school of sociology was the only thing of its kind apart from the less methodical training given at Settlements.

To-day the Universities have taken up the work of training men and women for social service, London, Bristol, Birmingham, Leeds, Liverpool, Edinburgh and Glasgow having departments of social science and administration. Certificates or diplomas are awarded to those passing the examination.

In the University of London Ratan Tata Department of Social Science and Administration, the course takes either one or two years, and consists of a combination of theoretical and practical work. Students as a rule attend the School for three days in the week for lectures and reading, while during the rest of the time they are engaged in some form of practical work. The student is attached to a C.O.S. office or a Children's Care Committee, or assists a health visitor or welfare supervisor; in the evening, perhaps, they take part in club work, or assist in the work of organising working women in trade unions. Some will be resident for the whole or part of the course in a Settlement, which offers experience in almost every kind of voluntary work, while at the same time affording opportunities of discussion with fellow-students or experienced social workers. At the School, in addition to lectures, an hour a week is devoted to private tuition under tutors, so that any difficulties that may arise in practical or theoretical work may be discussed.

We can now discuss in greater detail what are the subjects with which the social worker should be conversant.

First comes a knowledge of social conditions. Many students will have but little acquaintance with the conditions of life of those who do not belong to the class in which they have been brought up, or, although familiar with conditions of a particular district, know little of other places, and perhaps have not related what experience of social work they may have had to the general characteristics of the social system. This knowledge can only be acquired slowly and by actual practical experience. Six months' residence in a poor neighbourhood while engaged in some form of social effort will teach more than many books, nevertheless a good deal can be gained by reading. Thus, the survey of London made by Charles Booth and his collaborators, or of West Ham, York, Reading and other towns, by various authors, will supply a store of facts to the student, and reports of Government commissions and municipal authorities will supply statistics as to the character of the particular district in which the student is interested. They will at least show the student what to expect, and supply a mental framework which can be filled in from facts observed in the course of practical work, which then cease to be isolated observations and take their place in the picture of the place. Thus a knowledge of the conditions of the principal trades in a district will be of much help to anyone who is dealing with relief applications. For instance, a knowledge that the building trade is slack in the winter and that the district in which the student is working is a centre of that trade, will explain an increase of applications in the dull season.

Less statistical, but more descriptive of conditions of life and habit, are such books as "Across the Bridges," by Alexander Paterson, "The Town Child," by Reginald Bray, or Lady Bell's "At the Works," written by acute and sympathetic observers from without, while accounts from within, such as "The Children of the Dead End," by Patrick M'Gill, or "The Ragged Trousered Philanthropists," by Robert Tressail, give a picture of social conditions as seen by those who have been brought up in poverty and know from personal experience what it is to be hungry, houseless or unemployed.

Secondly, there is the study of social and industrial history. Our institutions have their roots in the past, and the causes of our present discontents must be sought not only in our own failings, but in the sins of omission and commission of our predecessors. Few people realise how ephemeral are many of our present-day conditions; people who pride themselves on being old-fashioned and sticking to the ways of their ancestors seldom go back more than a generation or two. Unless we go back and study the way in which this country has developed from an agricultural and comparatively isolated community into a world-centre of commerce and industry we shall not understand the problems that we are now trying to solve, or the reasons for the development of social theories. History as taught in the schools is largely political, and even so does not in many cases occupy a very prominent place in the school curriculum, while the social condition of the people at various epochs is apt to be subordinated to accounts of wars and rivalries of political parties. I remember that when I was at a school where history was rather better taught than elsewhere I learnt but little of social movements; Chartism was chiefly remembered by the fact that some of the signatures to the great charter were false; trade unionism was not mentioned, and industrial history was mainly an affair of overseas expansion and the acquisition of colonies. There was, too, a curious reluctance to deal with the nineteenth century, respectable history stopping short at 1815. Things may be better to-day, though I am not too sure, as schools are apt to be somewhat conservative.

It is not suggested that it is necessary for the student to be deeply versed in the manorial system or in the history of our fiscal arrangements, but a general knowledge of industrial development and social progress before the industrial revolution both at home and abroad is needed, while a more detailed knowledge is required after that.

Especially important are those movements that are powerfully affecting us at the present time, the causes that led to the trade union and co-operative movements, the history of factory legislation, the story of the chartist agitation, and the various social reform movements and their objects all require to be known.

The industrial structure of the country, foreign and home trade, the position of the country as a unit in the world economy, and the relations of capital and labour, are vital to a clear understanding of our position to-day.

Thirdly, there is economic science. Here again it is not possible for the social student to become in the short time at his or her disposal a profound economist. A working knowledge of the history of economic thought and the general principles of political economy are all that can be obtained. For it is not so much the abstract questions, theories of value or problems of currency and finance that will be of most use, but economics viewed from the social standpoint of the effect of economic laws on the life of the people.

Fourthly, the student must understand the structure of central and local government, particularly the latter. Formerly the Poor Law was the one subject on which all social workers were expected to be well informed, but to-day, while it is necessary to know the history of the English Poor Law (and in the Reports of the 1909 Commission a very valuable collection of information and comment on relief problems is to be found), more important is the general idea of English

Local Government, and the provision made locally for various services. In this, as indeed in all study, it is desirable to read something of foreign systems and experiments, so as not to take an insular view. While on the one hand there is sometimes a too great readiness to suggest the application of methods successful abroad to our own problems, on the other hand there is the danger of forgetting that other countries have their contributions to make to the solution of difficulties common to all societies at a similar stage of civilisation.

The machinery with which the social worker has mainly to deal to-day is controlled either by local and central authorities or by voluntary societies, and none of these must be neglected. The study of the history of voluntary effort in the past is valuable, not only as a history of thought on social matters, but as affording object-lessons as to what to seek for and what to avoid, for past failures often teach as much as past successes. Anyone who takes up social work will soon find himself in touch with all kinds of agencies represented by various alphabetical combinations, M.O.H., C.C.H.F., I.C.A.A., J.A.C. and J.O.C., so that even from the point of view of saving time a careful study of the principal agencies operating in a particular sphere of work will save much time.

Fifthly, social philosophy. It has already been pointed out that it is necessary for the social worker to look at things as a whole. There are plenty of people who shun abstract thought, who go on working without ever relating their activities to any general philosophy of life. It is, of course, necessary to have a limited and immediate objective, but this should form part of a scheme of social life to which one is striving to attain. Social philosophy will show us the relative importance of the various bits of social machinery that we are endeavouring to work, and will explain to us attitudes of mind of other people in the past or the present that would otherwise seem inexplicable. During the course of study the student will gradually find his own social philosophy, will see things as a whole and in relation to the general human process, with his eyes upon the goal at which he is aiming, while he will at the same time be able to appreciate the points of view of others.

Sixthly, there is social psychology. The study of the modes of thought of the individual and the group. Every social worker should be a practical psychologist, for he is working among men and women, and to arrive at some comprehension of what are the motives that are influencing them for good or ill, and what effect on the minds of individuals certain forms of activity will bring about, is part of his task, and not the least important part. Much of the failure in the past is a failure to estimate rightly the effect on individuals of particular actions, especially the effects of charitable action. To take an instance, what is the psychological effect of insuring a man a minimum of subsistence? Will it tend so to relieve his mind of worry that he will be able to develop his personality better, or will it remove a necessary stimulus, and lead to his stagnation? This is the kind of question that is raised to-day, and which has not yet been answered.

Again, in the smaller questions of detail, the study of the minds of the people with whom you are dealing and of human beings generally will prevent many mistakes. To give an instance, many religious bodies make the mistake of trying to bribe people to come into their churches by offering them pecuniary or material advantages. This is, I think, a profound mistake in the estimation of human nature. I know one club where as a condition of taking part in football, entertainments, and the other recreational activities the boys all had to attend a Bible Class, with the natural result that the class was very unpopular. At another club admission to the Bible Class was limited, and made the reward of good conduct, so that it became an object of ambition to be admitted. A third offered coffee and buns to all who would attend the mission, with the result that it was held in the utmost contempt.

I knew one club manager who maintained that every boy should always feel that the manager had his eye on him, while another trusted to the boys' honour and left them largely to themselves; the discipline of the second club was far the best.

In the larger movements, besides, an appreciation of the feelings underlying action saves much prejudice; people who get very angry over the one-man strike fail to understand the psychology of the trade unionist.

This appears a somewhat formidable list of subjects, but it is really only a minimum. Almost every sort of knowledge in fact will be useful to the social worker, and while it is not contended that good work has not been done by those who have not studied these subjects, yet it can be claimed that their success was not due to their ignorance but in spite of it. A strong personality will work wonders, but the more forcefulness is combined with thought and knowledge the better. We claim then that theoretical training is necessary, but not more so than practical; the two should go hand-in-hand, so that the problems encountered in practical work may be related to the theoretical principles studied, and the latter illuminated by living examples.

Most important of all is discussion with fellow-students and experienced workers, which can be obtained in the University common-room or at a Settlement, when experiences can be exchanged and rival theories discussed. It is a great advantage if, as at some Universities, the classes are attended by people drawn from various social strata. If the Oxford or Cambridge graduate, the young trade-union leader, the civil servant, and the business man attend the same courses and belong to the same debating societies, there is a likelihood that all will take wider views and obtain a better understanding of the human side of the problems with which they are dealing.

It would be well if all social workers would realise the need for now and again refreshing their knowledge in the light of new facts that have come to light, or new theories that have been formulated. It is easy to get so immersed in the details of work that little or nothing new is read; old methods are followed that have become obsolete, while new suggestions are misunderstood.

Vacation schools and summer schools afford this opportunity, but often, quite naturally, the tired social worker desires in the holidays to get right away from the circle of ideas with which he or she is familiar when at work. I think the habit of overwork is one to be guarded against by social workers; few of them are as indispensable as they think, and by taking some respite from work and attending classes or discussions or simply reading, they will be doing better work for the cause they have at heart than by sticking too close to their practical duties.

A word of warning might not be out of place to the young social worker who has completed a course of training and obtained a certificate, against taking up an attitude of superiority to the older workers who have been engaged in practical work for many years. They may be back numbers, but it is tactless to let them know that you think so, and they can easily retort that the young worker is inexperienced, as, indeed, is generally the case.

We have said above that the social worker has as much to learn as to teach, and there is one doctrine of the trade-union movement that should be thoroughly learnt by social workers and would-be philanthropists, to say nothing of those on central and local governing bodies, and that is the doctrine that a fair day's work demands a fair day's pay.

There are a great many cases of sweated social workers to-day. A local authority or a charitable society will think nothing of asking for a highly qualified lady, very likely with a University education, at a wage that is barely if at all sufficient to support life, a wage which would be indignantly rejected by a skilled worker in other walks of life ; if the work is worth doing and requires a paid worker, the pay should be such as will afford a full life to that worker.

Several reasons are suggested for this low pay, one that it is a charity and subscriptions are hard to get in ; but no trade unionist would admit this as a valid reason for paying a low wage. Another is that the work is attractive, a labour of love, and a reward in itself. This might be a good argument if carried out throughout the community, but in practice one does not find that the most unpleasant jobs are best paid—on the contrary. Other reasons put forward are the usual economic ones, that the woman is only working for pocket-money, and is really supported by parents or out of private means. I think the real reason is that the desire to work for something greater and more absorbing than mere private profit has created a big supply of social workers, and that this desire for social service is deliberately or unconsciously exploited against the interests of the social workers and also of the work.

It is generally admitted to-day that very low wages are economically unsound, and I believe that this is quite as true of the social worker as of any other.

There is still a survival of the ascetic ideal that the social worker should mortify the flesh, dress in dull—generally black—raiment, and take his or her pleasure sadly. I believe this to be thoroughly unsound. Social workers should not be segregated into a class spending their whole time in mean conditions of life, working long hours, and not mixing in the pleasures of others. They are entitled to as much pleasure as any one else, and if they stick merely to their work, living, let us say, in the east, and never going up west, they lose power, tend to become narrow and dull, and so cease to be as efficient as they might be. I hold that it is the duty of every one who sits on local or central authorities, or committees of charitable organisations, to see that their employees are well paid. I think it is time that social workers recognised this themselves, and that it behoves those with private means to realise that others have to live on their salaries, and that it is up to them not to "blackleg" them, but to work with them in order to establish a recognised standard and not leave them to the higgling of the market.

Probably the real remedy is in an increased recognition of the value of their work, and until this is evoked their wage will be low like that of the teacher, because the community does not recognise that their work is as valuable as that of the stockbroker or lawyer.

CHAPTER VI

RELIGIOUS AGENCIES

As has already been pointed out the religious impulse is one of the most powerful incentives to social service, and in this chapter an endeavour will be made to describe the social work of the various religious denominations, and to estimate their contribution to the solution or complication of social problems, noting how the conception of the attitude of organised religion to social matters has changed from time to time.

In the days when religion was the principal tie between man and man, when in England the Church was co-extensive with the nation, it was hardly possible to draw a line between religious and social activities. Religion was so closely interwoven into the texture of social life that the Church taught not only morality but economics, and religious observances were constantly brought to the attention of the ordinary man and woman, instead of as in modern days being confined to the week-end. The old Guilds that formed the structure of society in the mediaeval cities were as much religious as economic; they had their patron saints and their particular churches and chapels, and their acts of charity were as much religious as civil, while the monastery was an economic unit. Its inmates cultivated land, pastured flocks and herds, and carried on industry, quite as much as they said masses or relieved the poor. The parish church was used for civil business as well as for public worship, and indeed the ecclesiastical unit has formed the basis for our present local governing areas. A man's whole life was brought into contact with religion at every turn.

It was only after the Reformation and the emergence of rival sects that religion became separated from men's other occupations, and that the idea of religion as the possession of the individual began to compete with the idea of a religious community that was in fact only the people viewed under one particular aspect. It is not necessary here to examine in detail the evolution of the various religious bodies that exist to-day, but we must note that in course of time various causes have operated to deflect the churches from direct social service, and that the conception of the church as an instrument for social work has only arisen again comparatively recently.

To begin with the Church of England, we may note the deadening effect of the eighteenth century, and the growing gap between the parson and his poorer parishioners. Here and there the faithful priest was found, little above his congregation socially, and passing rich on £40 a year, who continued the old tradition of the Church, whereby the priest was not only the spiritual father of his people but their active helper and friend. But, in the main, the country parson became either a sort of squire or a hanger-on of the landed classes, performing his duties perfunctorily and with little care for the social needs of his parishioners. Very often he was an absentee and the duties were performed by a wretchedly paid curate. As the clergy became more and more identified with the wealthy, so the gulf widened between them and the poor, and the attitude of the parson was not so much that of a friend, as that of a condescending benefactor, or perhaps a censor of morals. The kind of life that was expected from the parson at the beginning of the nineteenth century can be well judged from the pages of Jane Austen. Doctor Grant in "Mansfield Park" was probably a fairly ordinary specimen, and the general idea of the town clergy is shown by Miss Crawford's description to Edmund of the parson as a man who had merely to preach two sermons a week. It is generally agreed that the eighteenth century was a period of great spiritual stagnation in the Church, and the benevolent enterprises undertaken during its course owed less to the religious impulse than to the philanthropic ideas of the philosophers. One particular form of social activity should, however, be placed to the credit of the eighteenth century cleric, and that was his service as a Justice of the Peace, which meant then not merely judicial but administrative work. Many of the County Magistrates were clergy, and were on the whole distinguished for their integrity and sense of duty at a time when the standard of those administering public affairs was not high. It must, however, be remembered that their attitude during the great changes brought about by the Enclosure Acts was as narrow as that of the laymen, and their activities against political reformers as unscrupulous and bigoted. It is with the coming of the industrial revolution and the mass of new social problems arising therefrom, that the indifference of the Church to the misery and injustice around them became most clearly evident. The clergy as a whole were against all efforts towards social reform that seemed likely to menace the privileged classes of society to which they belonged. As Lord Shaftesbury, himself the most notable example of the religious motive in social service, said of his struggle to obtain factory legislation, "In very few instances did any millowner appear on the platform with me; in still fewer the ministers of any religious denomination. At first not one, except the Rev. Mr. Bull of Bierley, near Bradford: and even to the last very few, so cowed were they (or in themselves so indifferent) by the overwhelming influence of the Cotton lords. I had more aid from the medical than from the divine profession."

The general attitude was based partly on the mistaken economics of the day, and partly on a conception of society that, though not often avowed, can still be found in certain classes of society, the comfortable doctrine that things as they are are right. It was explained to the "Lower Orders" by Wilberforce, "That their more lowly path has been allotted to them by the hand of God, that it is their part faithfully to discharge its duties and contentedly to bear its inconveniences: that the present state of things is very short: that the objects about which worldly men conflict are not worth the contest: that the peace of mind which religion offers indiscriminately to all ranks affords more true satisfaction than all the expensive pleasures which are beyond the poor man's reach: that in this view the poor have the advantage: that if the rich enjoy more abundant comforts, they are also exposed to many temptations from which the inferior classes are happily exempted: that having food and raiment they should be therewith content, since their situation in life, with all its evils, is better than they have deserved at the hands of God, and finally that all human distinctions will soon be done away and the true followers of Christ will all, as children of the same father, be alike admitted to the possession of the same heavenly inheritance." It is this doctrine of other-worldliness that accounts for very much of the hostility of the more thoughtful members of the working class to the established church, and also accounts for the peculiar indifference of the Church to the evils of modern Industrialism. The attitude of mind expressed in the extract given above has changed during the course of the nineteenth century, during which we may notice four movements in the Church that had powerful effects on its attitude towards social questions. The first is the Evangelical movement, which was really the result of the preaching of Wesley and Whitfield penetrating among those who did not desire to withdraw from the establishment. The movement includes several different streams of thought, embracing not only such a man as Wilberforce, who combined extreme solicitude for black slaves with complete indifference to the wrongs done to white workers at home, and Shaftesbury, whose reforming zeal carried him far beyond the narrow tenets of the sect.

To a certain amount of practical philanthropy and a conviction of the need for a reformation of manners of the poor, went a strong low Church piety that recalled to some extent the Puritans of former times, and thus, among the practical workers, can be claimed Howard, Mrs. Fry and Shaftesbury, who take a high rank among the exposers of abuses, and the members of the Clapham sect, who were more noted for their advocacy of anti-slavery and foreign missions, and for a somewhat condescending philanthropy, than for reforming zeal at home.

Their note was one of individualism, the saving of the soul of the sinner rather than the alteration of the conditions of life of the poor. Their attitude was that of those who have a higher morality, and are oppressed with the wickedness rather than the misfortunes of the poor, and while indulging in charitable actions themselves, they took up the attitude shown in the quotation from Wilberforce that the poor must look for their reward in another world. In this way the evangelicals contributed to the prejudice against the Church which may still be found, for not unnaturally it was regarded as an organisation for keeping the poor in their place, and persuading them to remain quiet in this world for the benefit of the rulers of it. That a good deal of the charity of this period was inspired more by fear than love can hardly be denied, the fear of revolution inherited from those who saw the French Revolution was present to their minds, and in every agitation for better conditions they saw the red terror raising its head in their own country. The provision of soup was a method of keeping the poor quiet, and Societies founded at this time, while no doubt not entirely deficient in the spirit of Christian charity, were to a large extent fulfilling the precept, "Feed the Brute," while educational endeavours were directed to the same end, that the poor might order themselves lowly and reverently to all their betters. Charity in the opinion of persons like Hannah More was an act of exceptional kindness on the part of the rich. Referring to a famine she tells some poor women, "Let me remind you that very scarcity has been permitted by an all wise and gracious providence to unite all ranks of people together, and to show the poor how immediately they are dependent on the rich, and to show both rich and poor that they are all dependent on Himself. I leave you to judge what would have been the state of the poor of the country in the long distress and scarcity, had it not been for your superiors. We trust the poor in general, especially those that are well instructed, have received what has been done for them as a matter of favour not of right, if so, the same kindness will, I doubt not, always be extended to them wherever it shall please God so to afflict the land." The school did, however, set up a standard of philanthropic effort that has endured among many of the families that belong to it, for the movement was in essence confined to certain middle or upper class families.

On the other hand Lord Shaftesbury was of a very different type, and combined the agitator and the social worker. The leader of the agitation for factory legislation and one of the pioneers of practical work among London street lads, for whom he founded the Ragged School Union, he left an enduring mark on the social history of England, and by his association with all kinds of Church activities in which his social rank added to his personal character rendered him prominent, he familiarised the mind of a large section of the Church with the idea of social reform. That a peer, a conservative and a churchman, should lead the attack on the abuses of the factory system, not from an abstract economic principle of State control, but from the effect of a knowledge of actual conditions, and should be prepared to work with radicals and atheists to attain his end, showed people that it was not only the have-nots who clamoured for reform, but that the Church had its duty to perform in endeavouring to obtain social justice. Religion in him, instead of leading to contentment with conditions in this world in the hope of recompense in another, led him to judge conditions as he saw them in the light of Christian teaching, and to condemn them as not in accordance with the spirit of the Gospel.

The second great change of thought was that brought about by the Oxford movement. Although not directly social in its inception and rather concerned with matters of faith, doctrine, and Church government, yet by the new energy it brought to the Church and the higher standard of parochial duty it demanded from the clergy, the movement led to the Church regaining to some extent its former position in the life of the nation. The new High Church parson was very different from the old Church and State Tory, and the insistence on the church as a divine society counteracted the extreme individualism of the low church school. The mediaevalism connected with the Catholic revival turned the thoughts of some back to the earlier life of the nation, and dissuaded them from the conception of modern industrialism as the last word of civilisation. It is due primarily to the Oxford movement that the High Church man to-day is as likely to take a keen interest in social work as his low church brother, and indeed it is the extreme high churchmen who are the most outspoken in their demands for social justice.

The third and most important movement was that of the Christian Socialists, who were in the main adherents of the Broad Church movement. The most prominent were Kingsley, Maurice, Thomas Hughes and J. M. Ludlow. It is not easy to estimate to-day the change in social outlook brought about by their work.

The idea of clergy being radicals and reformers, understanding the purpose of trade unions and frequently sympathising with them in their industrial struggles, denouncing housing evils, exposing the sweater, and preaching the possibility and necessity of re-establishing society on a basis of co-operation instead of competition, is familiar to us to-day, when a certain Dean has warned the clergy of the danger of becoming court chaplains to King Demos. But at the time when Maurice and Kingsley first called themselves Christian Socialists the need was to warn the clergy against being chaplains to King Mammon. Hence the shock administered by the writings and actions of the Christian socialists was extreme.

In a sermon preached in 1851, Kingsley spoke out : " I assert that the business for which God sends a Christian priest in a Christian nation is to preach freedom, equality and brotherhood in the fullest, deepest, widest meaning of those three great words ; that is as far as he does so he is a true priest, doing his Lord's work with his Lord's blessing on him ; that in so far as he does not he is no priest at all, but a traitor to God and man. . . . All systems of society which favour the accumulation of capital in a few hands, which oust the masses from the soil which their forefathers possessed of old, which reduce them to the level of serfs or day-labourers, living on wages and on alms, or deny them a permanent stake in the commonwealth, are contrary to the Kingdom of God which Jesus proclaimed."

It can easily be understood that doctrines of this kind proved rather strong meat for the average Church congregation and caused demands for Kingsley's inhibition, indeed even to-day they would very likely cause protests and lessen the preacher's chance of a living.

But the Christian socialists did much more than preach. In the co-operative and trade union movements, both at that time far less respectable than to-day, they took an active part, lending the weight of their names and giving help and advice. The evil of sweated labour was denounced in "Alton Locke," the condition of the agricultural labourer in "Yeast," and the agitation for sanitary reform which, dull subject as it sounds, was the first step in the reform of conditions of town life, owes as much to the advocacy of parsons as of doctors.

That the work of the Christian socialists influenced the clergy and the attitude of churchmen towards social problems is much; but yet another valuable service was rendered by them not only to the Church but to the nation. In continental nations the union of political and industrial democracy with anticlericalism is one of the marked features of social life. It is true that there are Christian socialist movements on the Continent, but these, if not actually concealing under a specious title some other object such as anti-semitism, are forms of counter attack against social democracy. That in this country organised labour is not hostile to Christianity, and that it has not entirely lost all faith in the churches as instruments of social justice, is due in the main to the Christian socialists.

At one time it looked as if the aggressive secularists had captured the leadership of the advanced movement among the workers, but the fact that prominent leaders of religious thought were not only not hostile but favourable to the claims of the workers for a wider life, has prevented such a division between Christianity and organised labour as may be seen on the continent. It is one example out of many in English life of the permeation of opinion from one camp to another.

The fourth movement is that of our own time, whereby the ideas of the Christian socialists (who were never more than a small group, their importance resting on the high qualities rather than the numbers of their adherents), have spread through the Church, affecting it in numerous ways. Thus, the more extreme views of the former movement were revived by the members of the Guild of St. Matthew and are represented by the Church Socialist League. (It may be noticed that the largest socialist body in the country has for some years had a beneficed clergyman on its executive.) The practical reforming spirit is represented by the settlement movement, and the foundation of missions which work on the same line as settlements, and by the Christian Social Union. This body, which is specially associated with the late Canon Scott Holland, has been a considerable influence in causing church people to study social questions, and seek for their solution in the light of Christian teaching. Inclusive rather than exclusive, it has served as a point of union for church people of different views. In particular it has served to bring prominently before their minds their duties as citizens and especially as consumers. Sweated labour has been one of its particular objectives. Endeavours have been made to freeze out the sweater by the publication of white lists giving the names of firms that provide good conditions, but the realisation of the impotence of the consumer to enforce his will has led to the closer study and the support of measures such as wages boards. Its members are urged to give service of whatever kind they can.

In the Church generally the study of social questions has been advanced by study circles and discussions, especially at congresses such as the Pan-Anglican, and opportunities have been given for the hearing of speeches from various points of view. Recently the Archbishops' Commission has reported on the relation of the Church to social and economic questions, and, as an example of the modern outlook of the Church to-day as compared with that of a century ago, I cannot do better than quote the conclusions of the Committee on Christianity and Industrial Problems (1918), "We cannot therefore agree with the view sometimes expressed which would allow Christians to take for granted the general economic arrangements of Society, and would confine their attention to supplementing incidental shortcomings and relieving individual distress in the belief that if men will live conscientiously within the limits of established industrial arrangements, without seeking to modify them, the result will be such a Society as can be approved by Christians. Nor can we accept without large qualifications the suggestion that the attempt to modify them is impracticable on the ground that any other arrangement is 'contrary to human nature.' We recognise indeed that the large changes which are necessary must be carried out gradually in a spirit of tolerance and mutual forbearance. But we think that it is precisely the general economic organisation of Society which is, in some respects, defective. That the efforts of Christians should be directed not merely to attacking particular evils as they arise, but to discovering and removing the roots from which they spring, and that Christian teaching supplies a sufficient motive to make practicable any change which is right.

" It is not enough, therefore, merely to cope with those defects which have become so clamorous or sensational as to attract general attention, for by the time they are sensational they may have become almost incapable of peaceful removal. It is necessary to make such changes in the normal organisation of Society as may prevent them arising. The solution of the Industrial problem involves, in short, not merely the improvement of individuals, but a fundamental change in the spirit of the Industrial system itself. . . .

"The co-existence in modern Society of riches and poverty is the tritest theme both of the economist and of the reformer, and we do not desire to repeat a miserable and thrice-told tale. But we would urge our fellow Christians to ask themselves once more whether an economic system which produces the striking and, as we think, excessive inequalities of wealth which characterise our present Society is one which is compatible with the spirit of Christianity or in which a Christian community ought to acquiesce."

There could hardly be a greater contrast between this extract and that given above from Wilberforce. Between the two lies the whole social experience of the nineteenth century, and the whole distinction between the attitude of charity and social service.

Turning to the practical social work of the Church of England, we must recollect that the primary motive for social work may be either an endeavour to attract the indifferent to the Church's ministrations by helping them in their physical needs and by strengthening the bonds uniting those who are already members, an appeal to the soul through the body, or the fulfilment of the Christian ideal of charity. The majority of missions, settlements and charitable societies in this country, owe their foundation to members of the establishment, and a glance at the Charities Digest will show the extent to which the Church has devoted itself to the ambulance work of the community. But I would rather draw attention here to the everyday work of the clergy and members.

The parochial system with its resident clergy and band of helpers, missioners, deaconesses and district visitors, provides an admirable framework around which every kind of social work may be grouped, and serves to make known the wants of individuals to those in a position to assist them.

In a well worked parish where the area has been carefully mapped out with plenty of helpers, each with his or her own sphere of work, the every day needs of the less fortunate may be dealt with by the charitable as far as is possible in the most appropriate way. The abuse of charity is very easy and it is the continual personal knowledge of the administrators that prevents it occurring. The parochial organisation can provide a much needed nucleus for a system of mutual assistance. At least there is someone to whom people can go for advice, and though the ideal of a resident gentleman in each parish smacks rather of patronage, yet in many a village the local parson is still the natural adviser of his parishioners.

The extent to which this is the case, varies naturally with the personality of the individual, but it is right that the large amount of social work performed by the clergy and the active members of the congregation should not be allowed to pass unacknowledged. To the local parson the social investigator and reform enthusiast is indebted for much useful information and sometimes help.

In connection with the church are generally clubs for boys and possibly for girls, men and women, some of which may be run by the clergy, some by his helpers; indeed the number of such social activities has become so great that complaint is sometimes made that the clergy have not enough time for their spiritual duties. In the towns the clergy are expected to serve on numbers of committees, and anyone of experience will know how largely such organisations as guilds of help, care committees, and relief societies are dependent on the local knowledge and active help of the clergy of all denominations.

There are two chief drawbacks to the social work of the Church. The first is its general reputation as a class church run by the rich in their own interests and drawing its clergy from one class only. Many will be inclined to say that this is as false as the current idea that the Church is supported out of the rates and taxes, but both views are widely prevalent.

A boy will say to you of the vicar in a poor district, "Look at him, he lives in a fine house and goes away for a holiday every year. What does he know about us?" Of course in many cases this is untrue, in fact, in many cases to-day the clergy are paid miserable stipends and are really sweated workers, but the point is that this view is widely held, especially by the more thoughtful of working men and women. There is a suspicion of patronage about the Church that is widely resented. Thus a woman will say, "I would not demean myself to go to a mother's meeting. I may be poor but thank God I haven't come down to that yet." This idea of class distinction vitiates much of the work of the church.

To show that this is not anti-clerical prejudice I will

quote from a communication sent by the present Bishop of Southwark to the Archbishops' Inquiry into Christianity and Social Problems.

"We clergy, with our public schools and universities behind us, look at political and social questions from a different angle from that of the vast mass of the working class. Instinctively and often unconsciously, our own past training and education make us critical of, or indifferent to the social problems.

"We cannot feel about them so deeply as the working class. The matters at issue in trade disputes are often quite unintelligible to us, while to the working class they are of vital importance. Words like 'hunger' and 'unemployment' connote to us something very different from what they do to the men who have actually experienced want. And I believe that the reason why the Church has so often been indifferent to social reform—and more than that has so often been found on the wrong side—is that we clergy, through our previous training, lack the imagination to see all it means for those who are suffering from social injustice. Men who have been brought up in the hard school of manual labour and poverty would instinctively sympathise with their class in this matter, as we, as a whole, instinctively sympathise in our hearts with the employers."

It is difficult for an institution to live down its past. Working men know that till recently, whatever may have been the position of individual clergy, the Church as an institution has been opposed to all their claims for better conditions, and that its most prominent lay supporters were, as a class, their political and economic opponents.

The second drawback is one which it shares with other

religious denominations, that of its connection with almsgiving. This is due to the first motive mentioned above, the desire to attract people to its services by offering material benefits. The connection of the clergy with any social reform movement has always been suspect to some on this ground, that they had no real interest in, let us say, housing reform or the abolition of sweating, except the hope of enticing people into their confession. More serious in its bad social effects was the system, not so prevalent now as formerly, of making attendance at church a qualification for gifts of money, blankets or grocery tickets. At the time when this form of pauperisation was at its worst it was the religious organisations that were mainly responsible. The attempt to distinguish between deserving and undeserving puts a premium on hypocrisy, the old woman who was always so regular at church got the blankets and the recommendation from the vicar. The result was that the weaker and less self-reliant people were demoralised, while the more self-respecting held apart from the churches in disgust.

SOCIAL SERVICE AND THE FREE CHURCHES

The non-conformist Churches have as a rule a less closely organised system than the Established Church, and the absence of the parochial organisation tends to make the social activities of each chapel more dependent upon the individual character of the minister, and the principal members.

The older non-conformist bodies drew their strength mainly from the middle classes in the towns, and the individualist tendencies of their creeds militated against their taking any very active part in social service, while their detached position as comparatively isolated and in some cases persecuted bodies, although it made the congregation a strong centre of social life, prevented them from looking so much at society as a whole. They have, however, an advantage over the Establishment in their more democratic constitution, in which the layman is given more power and responsibility, as a result of which a non-conformist chapel has been a training ground for public life. They have also not to contend with the prejudice that has been noticed above that makes men suspicious of the Church of England, and resent its patronage. The Wesleyan movement, that did so much to revivify religious life, had its effect not only on its own adherents but on the other Free Churches, which during the eighteenth century had become somewhat torpid. To the Wesleyan movement in particular must be attributed a very large share in the change in the manners, habits and morality of the working classes in the eighteenth century and those in the nineteenth. The miners, for instance, before the days of Wesley were regarded by most people as almost savages, and the fact that they are now as civilised as any other section of the workers must be attributed to a large extent to the work of the Wesleyan missionaries. In its inception the Wesleyan movement was directed far more to the reformation of the individual than to that of society, and indeed in the reforming movements of 1820-1830, while the accounts of the Wesleyans are conflicting, it would seem that on the whole their attitude of other-worldliness caused them to be on the side of law and order rather than that of the forces that were endeavouring to remould society. As Mr. and Mrs. Hammond explain in the "Town Labourer": "If we look into the life and teaching of this new religion we can see that the whole spirit of its mission was unfavourable to the democratic movement, and the growth of the Trade Union spirit. The Methodist movement was a call not for citizens, but for saints: not for the vigorous, still less for the violent redress of injustice, but for the ecstatic vision: the perfect peace of expectation. The brutal inequalities of life, the wrongs inflicted on man by man, the hardships of poverty and suffering, these vexations of a passing world were merely trials of faith for the true Christian, who could escape from them and sustain his soul with dreams of a noble and confidential companionship in this world, and of radiant happiness hereafter." On the other hand, the democratic organisation of the Free Churches, and particularly of the Wesleyans, has made them schools of training for public life, and the insistence on the importance of individual character has been of great value to all working-class movements. It must not be forgotten that such great organisations as the Trade Union, Co-operative Society and Friendly Society have only been built up on the basis of the integrity of character of numbers of individuals. A very large proportion of the leaders of working-class movements have been educated in the Free Churches, many indeed have been prominent in those bodies as local preachers, whereas very few have been brought up in, and still fewer have remained faithful to, the Church of England. This is due to the wider scope provided by the Free Churches for the laymen and the comparative absence of class bias. The Free Churches have for many years been the backbone of the Liberal Party, and as radical views have penetrated more and more within it, so the Free Churches have gradually changed their attitude from that of extreme individualism to a greater realisation of the importance of society.

The Free Churches, like the Church of England, have been forced in self-defence to take up social work as a method of endeavouring to attract people to their services, and their efforts in this direction have much the same characteristics as those already noted above. Many of their missions in the past and some at the present time have had a bad effect owing to the pauperising methods adopted, and they have fully taken their share in that competition in dole-giving which has had such a bad effect on some districts.

For the rest, their activities are much the same as those of the Church. They have taken their part in the Settlement movement, and especially in the poorer districts their churches have tended to become more institutional, and to be centres from which all kinds of social work is carried on. The Brotherhood movement has provided a common ground for those interested in religion and in social reform, and the provision of lectures on subjects of social interest has served to spread a knowledge of new ideas. In the Free Churches, too, there is a greater freedom of subject in the addresses delivered from the pulpit, resulting in the preaching of what their friends would call interest in public affairs, and their enemies politics in the pulpit. Generally speaking, in its social work the Free Church has been more successful in enlisting the services of the laity, mainly because they are not afraid of entrusting them with responsibility.

In any discussion of social service and the Churches a high position must be accorded to the Society of Friends, not from the number of its members, which is small, but from the high standard of citizenship that almost all of them exhibit. Although at one time somewhat hampered by extreme individualism, they have been found connected with very many of the chief social movements of our time. As a rule Quakers are well off, but they have always insisted on the responsibility of riches, both as to the method of their acquisition and of their spending. Many of the most fruitful experiments in the relationship of employers and employed, and in the humanising of the factory, have been made by members of this body; one need only recall the investigations of Mr. Rowntree and the experiments of Messrs. Cadbury at Bournville.

Their insistence on the responsibility of their members for their individual lives has steadily broadened into the responsibility for the community, and whereas in former times they were particularly noted for their work in such movements as that for the abolition of slavery abroad, they are now equally well known for the enthusiasm with which they have investigated conditions at home, and by experiment and agitation worked for reformation.

THE ROMAN CATHOLIC CHURCH

The Roman Catholic Church has always had a strong organisation for the undertaking of social work in its parochial system, and the religious orders supply it with a body of devoted workers. In this country as the Church of a minority and that minority containing a very large number of poor, especially in the great cities such as London and Liverpool, the need for special attention to charitable work has been emphasised and the desire to keep all its members in close touch with its religious ministrations has led to the foundation of many schools, orphanages, and homes of various kinds, supported by voluntary contributions raised from members of the Church. In this way the Catholic Church has to a large extent built up its own system of organisation for its members, apart from the provision made by the State. Thus special homes for children who have come under the Poor Law are provided by the Church, and sums are paid by the Guardians to these homes for the maintenance of the children, and they come under the ordinary inspection of the central authority.

In its outlook on social questions the Catholic Church is necessarily denominational, that is to say, that its views are subordinate to the general outlook on life of the Church. This has affected it in two ways: first it has, to a large extent, saved it from the influence of the extreme individualist outlook in social matters that was characteristic of much thought in the last century and from some of the tendencies to a merely material valuation of social life; but, secondly, it has led to a certain detachment from the life of the nation and from the aspects of social reform that belong to the realm of State action. On the Continent the connection of extreme views on social matters with direct anticlericalism had the effect of making Catholics somewhat apprehensive of being confounded with those whose immediate aims appeared to be consistent with catholic principles but whose outlook on religious matters appeared dangerous. Thus, despite the well-known encyclical of Leo XIII., "On the condition of the working classes," and the powerful help that Cardinal Manning rendered to the working classes by his attitude at the time of the dock strike in 1889 and by his interest in all social reforms, it is only recently that Catholic thought has been specially devoted to present-day social problems.

Interest in social problems has been much increased by the activity of the Catholic Social Guild formed in 1909 with the following objects: (*a*) To facilitate intercourse between Catholic students and workers, (*b*) To assist in working out the application of Catholic principles to our actual social conditions, (*c*) To create a wider interest among Catholics in social questions, and to secure their co-operation in promoting social reform on Catholic lines.

The guild has published a number of useful books on social questions from the Catholic point of view, and promotes the formation of groups and study circles for the examination of social problems, and for the education of its members. Besides this it also promotes the study of civics in Catholic secondary schools, and conducts examinations of the students.

By the provision of library facilities and book-boxes it strives to increase knowledge of social matters and promote the education of social workers. It has also taken part in interdenominational conferences with similar societies existing in other confessions, thus bringing its contribution into the common stock.

As far as practical work is concerned that of the Roman Catholic community is on the same lines as that of other bodies, clubs, settlements, and other institutions being supported, with the exception that the paid worker is generally a member of one of the religious orders. A good exposition of the Catholic attitude towards social matters will be found in "Christian Citizenship," by the Rev. Thomas Wright.

THE SALVATION ARMY

The Salvation Army, originally an extreme Evangelistic body started by General Booth with the object of converting the poorest and most degraded people by cheerful, lively and somewhat noisy methods, soon found itself driven to undertake social work. The condition of those among whom the Army conducted its operations, the poorest and lowest in the towns, was powerfully brought before the public by General Booth's book, "In Darkest England and the Way Out," although it was Mr. Frank Smith, then an officer in the Salvation Army, who first drew his chief's attention to the necessity of reinforcing the spiritual work with material supports.

There is no doubt that this book has had a very marked influence in calling attention to the conditions of slum life, but while some of the proposals made therein have been useful experiments, the results of the remedies for poverty applied by the Salvation Army can hardly be regarded as satisfactory. It is doubtful if the shelters provided have done much for the homeless: the existence of night shelters with cheap meals has the effect of making it possible for many to continue a mendicant existence, when it would have been better if they had found themselves unable to carry on, and thus had come to be dealt with by some more constructive method. The alliance of religion and relief puts a premium on hypocrisy, and although the army officials have great experience in detecting frauds, yet the somewhat theatrical methods of conversion and confession are likely to have a bad effect.

It was in recognition of the fact that more constructive work was necessary that the army endeavoured to relieve unemployment and strengthen the moral of the unemployed by opening workshops, where religious influences would be reinforced by regular work.

Unfortunately the economic basis of the scheme was unsound, for the turning out a cheap joinery undercut the regular workers in the trade, lowering the standard of life, and possibly throwing other men out of work, thus aggravating the very evil—unemployment—that it was designed to remedy. This is the objection to all such schemes where the wages of the trade are not paid, and where the business gets part of its support from charitable sources. It then becomes, in fact, a parasitic industry, doing as much harm as the sweated trade carried on for profit. Far better conceived were the schemes for training the unemployed upon farm colonies so that they might become self-supporting and be able to take their place as workers on the land, either in this country or overseas. It must be recognised that prolonged unemployment is very demoralising, and that it is idle to expect those whose moral stamina has been undermined by casual work and insufficient food to become useful citizens and workers by the mere provision of work. Some form of training is necessary, and also some form of moral suasion, and the Salvation Army employs methods that are, at least in some cases, effective. The Salvation Army has also carried out emigration on a large scale, and in this it has been fairly successful, though it has not always avoided the danger of sending men out to places already overstocked with labour. On a review of the work of the Army as a whole one is inclined to think that its special work is the reclaiming of criminals, drunkards and fallen women rather than general dealing with the unemployed. Whatever may be thought of the methods of the Army and its success or failure, it is impossible to withhold one's admiration for the self-denial and devotion of its members. Its officers have penetrated into places that no other agency has touched, and it has provided a great deal of information about those who are most difficult to help, and who are frequently disregarded in schemes for the reconstruction of society. The Church Army, founded by the Rev. Wilson Carlile, is an attempt to do the same sort of work under the aegis of the Church, and it may be regarded as an expression within the Church of the forces that have made the Salvation Army and the Y.M.C.A.

Y.M.C.A.

Before the war the Y.M.C.A. was regarded by most people as an organisation that dealt mainly with the more respectable and well-behaved, not to say goody-goody youth of an anaemic type, providing for him a rather mild repast of religion and amusement, but with the advent of the war its activities were enormously extended, and in the provision of recreation tents and huts in camps at home and in the various theatres of war it did an enormously valuable social work.

The army is not exactly a school for saints, and it is doubtful if the general public yet realises the very dangerous social experiment of suddenly taking all the youth of the nation and sending them to camps and barracks far from all home influences and subject to every kind of temptation. That the Y.M.C.A. did much to counteract these dangers will not be denied by its bitterest critics, and any returned soldier will bear testimony to the advantage of having some place to go to when off duty and some opportunity of writing letters, etc.

The Y.M.C.A., profiting by its war experience, is now embarking on a social experiment of great interest.

It wishes to set up all over England a system of clubs for men, women and boys. This design is to meet the need, which is very much felt by those who have been in the army, for places where they can meet their fellows. It is impossible to live for some time in barracks or messes without acquiring something of a gregarious habit, and the man who has been demobilised feels the lack of companionship. In many districts the supply of clubs is hopelessly inadequate, and the public-house is almost the only alternative.

This experiment has already met with some opposition from the Churches, though it is a field where there is plenty of room for all, while the Y.M.C.A., being unsectarian, and having at its command a large body of skilled workers, would seem to be in a good position to fill this want, and there seems no reason why the active co-operation of the agencies already in the field should not be secured. The Churches have hitherto tended to thrust religion down people's throats, with the result that many are kept away; the average man does not want to end his evening with a service or even a prayer meeting, and does not like to take advantage of the hospitality of a club and then go out before the service. I think that if the services are kept strictly voluntary and unsectarian there is great hope that the movement will fill a want in English life that is to some extent filled by the café abroad and that certainly is not filled by the ordinary public-house in England. The Y.W.C.A. provides similar services for women.

Among other social agencies, the basis of which is definitely religious, reference may be made to the various Rescue societies and Prisoners Aid societies, and particularly to the most hopeful side of the work, that among the young delinquents.

SUMMARY

From the standpoint of the social worker there are three principal services that the Churches perform. The first is the inspiration that the Church gives to many to devote themselves to the service of others. The Churches should hold up a high ideal of service, reinforcing the appeal of society for all its members to labour for its benefit, with the conception that all their work is done for the greater glory of God. The social message of the Churches reinforces that of the State.

Complaints are sometimes made that the age is material, that social reform is too much directed to such things as increased wages, shorter hours of labour, better houses and the like, and some clergy are prone to lecture those who are conspicuously lacking in these things, for their absorption in matters that do not really make people better or happier. Whatever truth there may be in this, it is for the Churches to set up a high ideal, and it should be their special province of social work to keep ultimate aims before those immersed in practical affairs.

Secondly: the Churches form social nuclei in the somewhat chaotic conditions of modern life round which social activities can be grouped. One of the difficulties of social work to-day is the enormous size of the units into which society is divided, and the consequent loss of the feeling of neighbourhood and civic consciousness. In the city of two or three hundred thousand persons the local governing bodies are as far from the people as the central Government, still more in the big new suburbs or urban districts, and most of all in London. It is hard to be an enthusiastic citizen of Willesden or Croydon, West Bromwich or Islington; our political divisions have become too big and often do not represent anything inspiring. In a modern town few people know their neighbours, especially in the residential districts. In London only here and there, mostly in very poor districts along the riverside will be found any real feeling of neighbourhood. The parish or congregation can supply this gap and create that loyalty to an institution that produces self-sacrifice.

It is true that to-day the Churches are out of touch with the majority of the people, their services are scantily attended in most cases and confined largely to the middle and upper classes, and the experience of chaplains in the late war has given considerable cause for despondency among ministers of all denominations, yet too great an interest in social problems is not given as one of the reasons for the indifference.

Thirdly: there is the moral influence of the Churches on individuals not only in setting a standard for the ordinary man and woman, but in retrieving those who are morally defective.

However sanguine we may be as to the general goodness of humanity, and however confidently we may believe that a large proportion of crime is due to physical and mental defects, requiring rather the doctor than the parson or the prison warder, we have to remember the number of people brought up in bad surroundings or morally weak who must be dealt with as individuals, and to whom the method of moral suasion brought to bear through the Churches is most applicable. It is in these directions that the special utility of the Churches in social work is found. The child with a defective moral sense, the prostitute, the criminal, and the habitual vagrant may be moved by the ministrations of religion when other agencies would fail. The work of the Wesleyans in their reform of manners at the end of the eighteenth century, and the conversions effected by the Salvation and Church Armies in our own day, indicate the kind of service that can be rendered. The work is difficult, and to most people very unattractive, requiring great enthusiasm to support those engaged in it, and it is the religious motive that has in the past and will in the future recruit workers for this service.

CHAPTER VII

THE SETTLEMENT MOVEMENT

THE Settlement Movement in England that started in the early eighties of the last century may be said to have opened a new era in social service with the conception of its originators, that the chief thing needful was not the mere giving of relief, but an active sympathy and co-operation between classes that could only be gained by the well-to-do going down to the districts where the poor congregated and getting to know them as friends and neighbours.

The old English theory of society presupposes that in every district there will be a sufficient number of people able and willing to work for the community. The old system of local government rested on the basis of the unpaid work of the inhabitants themselves; thus the parish appointed its officers, the churchwardens, way-wardens, constable, etc., who carried out the duties of local government, and the idea was that each in turn undertook these communal burdens. This system was well suited to the old comparatively static conditions existing before the industrial revolution, when each village was an almost self-contained unit, with its hierarchy of classes, and its squire and parson, while in the towns the corporation or the leading citizens carried out similar duties.

With the opening of the nineteenth century, however, came large-scale production, the growth of huge new agglomerations of population in districts where there was no old-established civic spirit, with the result that the old organisation of the parish broke down. It was unfortunate that these great social changes came at a time when the system of town government had decayed, corporations and parishes had become the close preserves of little cliques, and public spirit was at a low ebb. For the first time in our history society splits up, and the masses are herded into special districts, segregated from the better classes and left with little or no government from above, while there was, as yet, no power to create an organisation from their own ranks. We are to-day quite accustomed to think of certain districts as working-class, upper-class, or middle-class, residential or industrial, but it is well to recall how novel is this situation, and how many of the evils of society to-day are due to this segregation. This evil was particularly great in London, owing to its great size and on account of the refusal for many years of the city corporation to take the responsibility for the government and well-being of the huge chaotic districts that had grown up around it ; thus the masses of the country were deprived of the essential of an orderly life, sound local government, and this reacted throughout on the physical, moral and mental condition of the people.

What is not seen is not noticed, and even to-day in London there are masses of people who know practically nothing of the districts that lie Across the Bridges or east of Aldgate, and still more who, if they have heard of them, have never been there : if this is true of places like Bermondsey, Stepney, Poplar, Bethnal

Green and West Ham, which have been extensively advertised, it is still more true of the less picturesque but equally dull London dormitories of Tottenham, East Ham, Leyton and Walthamstow. The London of the eighties was a very different place from what it is to-day. Its government was still in the hands of a number of small authorities, Vestries, Boards of Works, etc., and the unifying and reforming energies of the London County Council were yet to come. The housing problem was only just beginning to be tackled, and was as big a problem as it is to-day, with the absence of the experience now available to guide in its solution.

The great development of transport, trams, omnibuses and railways that has done so much to open up central London and enable its inhabitants to get further out had not taken place. The effects of compulsory education, which after nearly fifty years of experience we are now feeling in many little-realised ways, were then only just beginning to influence the younger generation, while University Extension was a new movement. The great awakening of trade unionism among the less skilled workers, which was to come as the result of the dock strike of 1889, had not ruffled the surface of the complacent, rather pacific and respectable movement of the middle of the nineteenth century, while the casual dock labourer and sweated woman worker were about to emerge into the light of day as typical products of unrestrained industrialism. Manners were far rougher; there were streets in East London that were unsafe to pass down at night, and the difficult, though on the whole law-abiding foreign element was, then as now, present as a complication.

Since the days of the early settlers conditions have changed very much, thanks to the efforts of reformers of all shades of opinion and of the workers themselves, and it is perhaps difficult for us to realise to-day all the novelty of the ideas of Arnold Toynbee, Canon Barnett and others.

The period that produced the Settlement movement was one when the interest of the educated classes had been powerfully turned towards a consideration of the social problem.

A new generation had sprung up who were not blinded by the material successes of industrialism to the ugliness and evil that it brought in its train.

Carlyle's attacks on the crude doctrines of the Manchester School and the vulgar standards of business, with his emphasis on the importance of the individual, and his attacks on shams and abuses, had cleared the air of much cant. Ruskin was denouncing the ugliness of life and preaching the doctrine, not merely of artistic beauty, but the need for re-creating the old joy of the craftsman in his work. His powerful attacks on the political economy of the day with its narrow interpretation of wealth and its gospel of cheapness, were restoring the idea of art as part of the life of the nation, to which every man had a right; not a sort of adornment for a drawing-room, a pleasing trimming to more serious business; and his teaching was having a double effect, not merely in the establishment of new standards of taste, but of a new, or rather a return to an old idea of a life which should be one of happiness and beauty dedicated to the service of God and man. And this new gospel was finding its finest expression in William Morris and his companions, who were led by their love of art to the conviction that the whole of the present civilisation was on a false basis, and that nothing but a return to a society based on fraternity instead of competitive selfishness could provide an environment in which art could again come to its own.

In the religious world the ideas of the Christian Socialists were being continued by the members of the Guild of St. Matthew, with its conception of the need for making the Church a social force, and its protest against the assumption that the existing order was in consonance with the ideals of the Founder of Christianity.

In the political world the enormous stimulus of the economic doctrines of Henry George was causing a revival of the Socialist movement, and the Social Democratic Society and the Fabian Society were coming into being, the one with its vigorous propaganda among the workers, the other with its investigation into conditions, its permeation of middle-class thought, and its provision of powder and shot for the use of the less educated denouncers of social injustice.

But perhaps the most immediate influence in formulating the ideas that produced the Settlement movement was the teaching and practice of T. H. Green at Oxford. His philosophy, with its emphasis on the right of every human being to a full opportunity of developing his faculties; and the need for ensuring the conditions under which those faculties could be exercised, together with his lofty conception of the duty of the citizen in the modern State, were allied to personal service in the routine of municipal life and in voluntary social effort. The young men of the University, such as Toynbee and his contemporaries, learnt their social philosophy from him and profited by his example. Edward Denison and Arnold Toynbee, by going to live in poor districts, really started the Settlement idea, though in both cases their early deaths removed them before they could see the fruit of their efforts. To Canon Barnett above all was due the practical inception of this movement as of so many others, for it was his experience as vicar of St. Jude's, Whitechapel, of what was the most urgent social reform for East London, at the time, that enabled the experiment to be successfully inaugurated.

It was then, when the movements and ideas that have done most to mould the social progress of recent years were in their full glow of early enthusiasm and hope, and when a new idea of the relationship between the various classes of society was beginning to penetrate the minds of thinking men and women, that the experiment of the Settlement was made.

Perhaps the best notion of what the founders of the Settlement movement aimed at can be gathered from the following extract from a speech of Canon Barnett to Oxford undergraduates, quoted by Mrs. Barnett in her life of her husband. "Enquiries into social conditions lead generally to one conclusion: they show that little can be done *for* which is not done *with* the people. It is the poverty of their own life which makes the poor content to inhabit 'uninhabitable' houses, and content also to allow improved dwellings to become almost equally uninhabitable. It is the same poverty of life which makes so many careless of cleanliness, listless about the unhealthy conditions of their workshops, and heedless of anything beyond the enjoyment of a moment's excitement.

"Such poverty of life can best be removed by contact with those who possess the means of a higher life.

Friendship is the channel by which the knowledge—the joys—the faith—the hope which belong to one class may pass to all classes. It is distance that makes friendship between classes almost impossible, and therefore residence among the poor is suggested as a simple way in which Oxford men may serve their generation. By sharing their fuller lives and riper thoughts with the poor, they will destroy the worst evil of poverty. They will also learn the thought of the majority—the opinion of the English nation—they will do something to weld classes into society." Here we have expressed the primary idea of the Settlement movement in England that has spread from London to the provinces and overseas to America. The movement has taken such strong root in the United States that it will be well to give here the idea of the Settlement as conceived by its greatest exponent in that country, Miss Jane Addams of Hull House, Chicago, who says:

"The Settlement then is an experimental effort to aid in the solution of the social and industrial problems which are engendered by the modern conditions of life in a great city. It insists that these problems are not confined to any one portion of a city. It is an attempt to relieve, at the same time, the over-accumulation at one end of society and the destitution at the other; but it assumes that this over-accumulation and destitution is most sorely felt in the things that pertain to social and educational advantages. From its very nature it can stand for no political or social propaganda. It must, in a sense, give the warm welcome of an inn to all such propaganda, if perchance one of them be found an angel. The one thing to be dreaded in a Settlement is that it loses its flexibility, its power of quick adaptation, its readiness to change its methods as its environment may demand. It must be open to conviction and must have a deep and abiding sense of tolerance. It must be hospitable and ready for experiment. It should demand from its residents a scientific patience in the accumulation of facts, and the steady holding of their sympathies, as one of the best instruments for that accumulation. It must be grounded on a philosophy whose foundation is on the solidarity of the human race, a philosophy that will not waver when the race happens to be represented by a drunken woman or an idiot boy. Its residents must be emptied of all conceit of opinion and all self-assertion, and ready to rouse and interpret the public opinion of their neighbourhood. They must be content to live quietly side by side with their neighbours, until they grow into a sense of relationship and mutual interests. They are bound to see the needs of their neighbourhood as a whole, to furnish data for legislation, and to use their influence to secure it. In short, residents are pledged to devote themselves to the duties of good citizenship, and to arousing the social energies which too largely lie dormant in every neighbourhood given over to industrialism. They are bound to regard the entire life of their city as organic, to make an effort to unify it, and to protest against its over-differentiation."[1]

Toynbee Hall, the first English Settlement, was founded by Canon Barnett, then vicar of St. Jude's, Whitechapel, and has to a large extent been the model of all subsequent ventures. Its essential characteristic is the gathering together of a number of men interested in social problems, who live a common life in a poor

[1] *Twenty Years at Hull House*, Jane Addams, p. 126.

district. The framework of the Settlement is not unlike that of an Oxford College, with its private rooms of residence and its common-room, dining-room, etc., in common, while close to it or in its near neighbourhood are grouped the various class-rooms, club-rooms, and offices, in which the residents carry on some of their various activities. At the head is the warden, whose business it is to keep up enthusiasm, direct the work of the residents, and by his experience guide the whole venture.

A movement started at the same time as the Settlement with many points in common was that of the Missions, some like Oxford House, with the definite idea of affording training in social work to those intending to take holy orders, others with their principal objective the strengthening of the religious life of a parish or chapel by the association of laymen with clergy, and yet others with the idea of creating a new centre of religious life where population had outstripped the former provision.

These Missions primarily appeal to those who are most concerned in spreading the Christian Gospel, and whose care for the minds and bodies of those they seek to influence is really mainly a way of approach to the soul, whereas Settlements such as Toynbee Hall and the Passmore Edwards, formed on a definitely non-sectarian basis, appeal to a somewhat wider range of interests, aiming to collect under their banner the enthusiast for art, literature, learning, industrial and social betterment.

The points of agreement are, however, far more marked than those of difference, and they can be grouped together as one phase of social activity with the one invariable characteristic of the residence in poor districts of those drawn from a more fortunate social stratum. The majority of Settlements and Missions have also this in common that they draw their support from schools or universities, their aim being two-fold, to interest and educate the members of the institution that supports them in the social problems of the time quite as much as to influence those among whom they work.

The characteristics of different Settlements will then be due less to differences of aim than to variations of environment, tradition, and the personalities of the leaders. While the general character of the work will be much the same in all, some will specialise in particular forms of social endeavour, thus the Passmore Edwards has devoted much attention to providing recreation for children, the Browning Settlement devoted itself particularly to the agitation for old age pensions, while Oxford House has mainly worked among boys. Some Settlements will confine themselves to practical work in alleviating distress, and assisting the people of the neighbourhood, others will combine this with research into industrial conditions. It may, however, be remarked that it is easier to retain a continuity of policy and an unity of effort in the avowedly religious Settlement than in the secular; for the changes in the former will be mainly those of method, whereas in the latter an altered attitude towards the social problem as a whole, on the part of most of those interested, may mean that fundamental alterations are necessitated.

SETTLEMENT WORK

The primary work of a Settlement is to be the centre for all the social work of a district. The aim of the residents should be to get into touch with all the forces that are engaged in endeavours to better social conditions or assist individuals ; thus the note of the Settlement should be catholicity. Here is the real difference between the Settlement proper and the Mission.

A Mission is necessarily primarily concerned with the interests of a particular denomination : its main object is to act as a support and rallying point for the adherents of a particular creed, and however broad-minded may be the men and women who are working there, it is almost impossible to escape a certain sectarianism and a certain narrowness. Those who support financially a Mission or a church or chapel Settlement will naturally demand that the atmosphere shall be definitely Church of England, Nonconformist, or Catholic, and those who come from without, adherents of rival creeds or perhaps owing allegiance to no creed, will feel a certain restraint in coming to the Settlement house ; their collaboration will be not complete. The idea of the first Settlement, despite the fact that its head was a beneficed clergyman, was inclusiveness.

Dealing then first of all with the undenominational Settlement, it is desirable that it should comprise residents and helpers of different social and political views. Its object is to get into touch with all social workers, and it is undesirable that all the residents should be Socialists or all Individualists, for discussion among the residents is one of the best methods of education that a Settlement affords. It is an attempt to create the atmosphere of the university, and the opportunity thus provided for the exchange of views is indeed one of the arguments for a life in a community, and discussion will be narrowed if rival points of view are not represented.

To the enthusiast all points of view but his own seem retrograde, but it is the business of the Settlement to assist in the expression of the great floating mass of social goodwill that exists in all classes, for if the Settlement is to do its work it must not be a select body of the socially conscious, but must try to influence those who are less awake to social evils.

A Settlement should, to my mind, be mainly a place for young men. There is need, it is true, for some one older and more experienced as warden, but even in his case the younger the better ; Canon Barnetts, who can keep their enthusiasm ever fresh and constantly review old methods in the light of new problems, are very scarce, and as it is of the utmost importance that the warden should be able to stimulate his residents and set them working, the younger he is the better.

Life in a community appeals to the young ; it is a continuation of the habits of school and college, but if indulged in too long is apt to distort the view. Just enough older men to give advice and ensure continuity of effort is all that is desirable, for older men and women in Settlements are apt to have stereotyped views and to tend to look back to the past instead of forward to the future.

The situation of a Settlement is one that requires great consideration. All places have their natural centres, and there is the position for the Settlement. It must be well among the people that it wishes to serve, that is the first consideration ; the second is that it should be well served with lines of communication to the districts from which it will draw its workers, and to which they can easily go when they want to mix with their friends of their own class. There is a tendency of some Settlement workers to bury themselves in their Settlements, which is I think to be deprecated. I do not believe in Settlements that remain on the borders of their districts; people who have been at work all day will not willingly turn out to go a long distance for a class or a club. It may not be so pleasant in the heart of the district, but it is no good trying to make the best of both worlds On the other hand, the quieter the better, for if some of the residents are students, and if classes, etc., are to be carried on, a position in a main thoroughfare, though good for advertisement, is bad for work. Settlements that have been established in a certain district must be prepared if necessary to go elsewhere; some much advertised slum districts become saturated with institutions, in others the population or the character of the district changes. It requires considerable determination to move, the force of sentiment and the influence of past residents will be all opposed to it, but there are few more pathetic sights than that of an institution that has lost its utility struggling on immersed in the traditions of the past.

The Settlement forms a good centre for charitable societies of all kinds, and it is very desirable that these should be accommodated with offices if possible: the local branches of the C.O.S., the Invalid Children's Aid Association, the Children's Country Holiday Fund, etc., should be found there, and it should be the meeting-place of the Guild of Help or Council of Public Welfare, and the natural centre for the various committees that spring up from time to time to deal with specific causes. At some Settlements rooms are provided for Friendly Society and Trade Union meetings in place of the usual public house, but as a rule it is best to steer clear of political meetings. If something in the nature of a common club-room can be provided, where those attending these meetings can meet and exchange views, it is all to the good.

One of the principal ideas of the Settlement movement is education. In former days the Settlements took the lead in the provision of continuation classes, or even provided classes for the elementary education of those who had not had the opportunity of going to school; but with the increase of the activities of the local education authorities these can better be given outside, and the educational work of Settlements is concentrated rather on university classes and the supplying of gaps in the facilities provided elsewhere.

Till quite recently Toynbee Hall continued to provide instruction in commercial subjects, partly because this had been one of the early services of the Settlement, partly because it was hoped to attract students who came for those classes to join also those which dealt with subjects of permanent educational value. In the early days of the University Extension Movement the Settlements formed a valuable centre, and though this movement has hardly fulfilled the hopes of its founders, and has become somewhat middle-class, yet it is still a Settlement activity. Much can be done in the provision of special classes for comparatively small groups, and in the formation of societies composed of residents and out-working people. Some will be dramatic, taking the form of Shakespeare Readings or Dramatic Clubs, producing plays from time to time; others are devoted to the study of literature or art. Parties will be taken out to the country to sketch or study natural history, or sometimes abroad to learn something of their neighbours overseas.

An instance of successful work is that of the Whitechapel Art Gallery, started by Canon Barnett, in which loan exhibitions are held and volunteers attend to explain the pictures. That this supplied a need is shown by the fact that in the first ten years some three million persons visited it. The number and variety of these educational classes and clubs depends on the finding of a sufficient number of residents with the special qualifications needed to make them a success.

Another advantage of the classes is the possibility of bringing down the greatest authorities in their own field of work to give addresses, thus bringing people in contact with the best thought of the day. This can also be usefully achieved through the agency of debating societies. The success of these largely depends on the choice of a chairman, for after their establishment there is generally evolved a group of habitues who are prepared to bore the meeting on any conceivable subject, and these require tactful repression. A good variety of debating club is the local parliament, though it is sometimes a little difficult to secure the due representation of all parties, while another is the free religious discussion in which a more serious atmosphere can be created than in the less formal encounters in the parks of the secularist and the Christian Evidence speaker.

Mention may be made here of the series of addresses on religion by leaders of Labour delivered at various times at the Browning Settlement in Walworth, which did much to clear away certain common misapprehensions engendered by a too close reliance on the daily newspaper as an exponent of the attitude of the working man to religion.

Settlements are rather prone to confine themselves to meetings of middle-class social workers alone, and the great number of these becomes a weariness of the flesh, whereas the admixture of other classes would tend to enliven the proceedings.

The advent of the Workers' Educational Association affords a good opportunity for making the educational side of the work a more living part of the Settlement. Residents can take small classes, the members of which are keen to learn, and from whom the tutor will learn much, and such classes might well be recruited from the boys with whom the resident has been brought into contact through the club or scout troup.

Work among boys and girls is the most attractive field for the young, and most Settlements have clubs either on the premises or in the surrounding districts for which residents are responsible.

Despite the number of years that recreation has been provided in clubs, the number of lads and girls who are quite untouched by the Club, Cadet, Boys' Brigade or Scout movements is still very great. I have heard of clubs that have a difficulty in getting members, but where this is so there must be something wrong, for any decent club will find itself with a waiting list. An important variant of the usual club is the mixed one, where boys and girls can meet for dancing, singing or other recreations, or for educational purposes. They are most important as places where the young man and woman can meet of an evening and become acquainted. The limited accommodation of the average home in a working-class district does not afford much opportunity for acquaintance to be formed, and a knowledge of each others' characters to be obtained. The alternative is walking out in very noisy public streets, or in the less frequented ones, that sometimes have their own dangers, so that the provision of such meeting-places is very desirable. In some towns where clubs are federated, dances are run by a central organisation for the benefit of the members of both sexes belonging to affiliated clubs, and Settlements might well do this in other towns.

Quite as important as clubs for the young are those for adults, particularly married women. For these latter it is essential that they should be close to the members' homes, for they have little spare time. The old type of mothers' meeting has fallen somewhat into disfavour, but there is a great need for the provision of places where women can meet and discuss affairs in general, as a substitute for the loneliness of those who keep themselves to themselves, or the gossip of those who do not.

It has already been said that much social work centres in the local authorities, and a resident can be of much use by giving his services. The average municipal body is none too well off for ideas, and the educated man or woman who has had greater opportunities than others of studying, not only what is done elsewhere at home, but the fruitful experiments abroad, can stimulate improvement by advice and expert knowledge. In some districts the main thing is the somewhat elementary one of getting disinterested councillors elected, but in most of the larger ones the keen resident will find plenty of support.

But Settlement workers can do far more than serve as councillors; they can get to know councillors of all parties and of all points of view, and influence them by ordinary conversation towards higher civic ideals, and the Settlement itself should be a place where information can be obtained. The Settlement library should be available to those responsible for local administration who wish to study the general principles and the detailed work of municipalities, and there should also be a store of information on the district and its needs, what has been done and what might be done.

The residents themselves can stimulate demand for better utilisation of existing facilities ; for instance they can survey all the available parks and open spaces, and make suggestions for their better use and watch for opportunities for their extension.

An active outside body can do much by carrying out these local investigations, providing at the same time powder and shot for reformers, and useful training for the younger residents, who will often be students at some university.

Nor is it only on local government affairs that this investigation can be advantageously carried out. At the present time the proper organisation of industry is a burning question, and while some will prefer to consider why certain individuals are poor, others will like to investigate the conditions in the industries of the locality, finding out why this industry is declining, why that pays such low wages, and whether another could not be removed from the district with advantage or a new trade introduced. An example of this work, though carried out by an individual in the main and not by a group, is Sir William Beveridge's well known study of under-employment at the docks, made when he was a resident at Toynbee Hall.

Another useful form of investigation is the district survey, a work particularly popular in American Settlements.

Apart from organised work there is much that residents in Settlements can do as individuals. In the earliest Settlements it was the ideal to establish relationships of real friendship between people of different classes, and this has been done by many. The best way is by taking an actual part in local organisations as an ordinary member, being careful not to arrogate to oneself any exceptional position on account of superior social status. The particular organisation will be dictated by the individual's tastes and capacities: the painter or sculptor may form art societies, or assist in bringing a knowledge of art to the many by arranging exhibitions, etc.; literary and dramatic societies are often already in existence, or can be formed, and here is scope for those with knowledge and enthusiasm, while of all the arts, probably music is most widely appreciated. Where classical literature or painting makes little appeal there will be found many who have a taste for classical music, even among those who would appear to be least likely subjects. I have known a very rough lad whose work was coal-heaving go up regularly to classical concerts all over London.

Broadly speaking, the idea is not so much to improve people by introducing them to culture, as by showing them the extent of the heritage of human achievement that can be enjoyed. Here is a work worth doing, the broadening of the interests of the mass of the people and the creation of new desires. At the present time hours are being shortened and the main motive behind the desire for reduced hours is for increased leisure and by the active minority for increased opportunities for development. Increased leisure requires wise use if it is to benefit the community; the old libel that increased leisure meant more time in the pubs and increased wages more custom to the publican, had a certain amount of truth in it at a time when the interests of the workers had been narrowed down, and when the possibilities of alternative enjoyments were restricted by lack of education. To-day, with the extension of education, there is no reason why this should be so, and those who wish to share the advantages they possess with others will find a ready response.

A further use of the Settlement is to form a place where all sorts of advice can be obtained. There are Settlements in poor districts that have this reputation, and in their neighbourhood whenever anything goes wrong, a domestic quarrel, an accident to a member of the family, or any question or difficulty, the first idea is to go and see Miss So-and-So. In cases like this the Settlement has become a well recognised part of the life of the district, but such a position depends mainly on the personality of a particular resident, and requires much time to establish.

A specialised part of the advice department frequently found in Settlements is the Poor Man's Lawyer, where one or two lawyers give up an evening or two a week to hear all applicants, and give free legal advice, and sometimes take up cases of hardship, or arrange with a good firm of solicitors to do so.

At first sight this might appear superfluous, or even a form of black-legging a hard-working profession, but advice is given to those who in any case could not afford a lawyer's fees, and the standard of the lawyer in a poor district is not apt to be a high one. This explains the general dislike of the lawyer, who is judged by the specimens with which working people come most in contact. I remember, on giving up practice at the bar, being congratulated by my friends in a poor district in much the same terms as would have been employed had I at last given up the drink.

The success or failure of a Settlement will largely depend on the personality of the head, and the position requires rather a rare combination of qualities, of which perhaps tolerance and enthusiasm are the chief.

A word has already been said as to missions and their separate functions. Some approximate very closely to Settlements, others are only offshoots of churches. The mission suffers perhaps from a disadvantage in that it is less apt to attract the young, especially the young men, who are not often enthusiastic in taking part in the directly propagandist work of a church, unless they are intending to become clergy, in which case their stay will probably be short, and they will be lost to the mission owing to taking up work elsewhere, while the Settlement can often rely on the interest and work of old residents years after they have left.

The Settlement has a useful function to perform in the sphere of international relations, for nations at the same stage of economic development have much to learn from each other as to the various means adopted in them to meet the same problems, and the Settlement forms an ideal place of meeting. It is not so much a knowledge of the organisations for social work and their structure, although this can be gained to a great extent from books, that is needed, but an interchange of ideas. It can best be obtained by living a life in common with people of a different country or race who are interested in the same subjects. Thus at Toynbee Hall in particular, there is generally some one from a foreign country or from the colonies or the United States who is studying our social arrangements, while at the same time affording the residents there a glimpse of how men's minds are moving overseas. If this plan of residents from Settlements in one country visiting those of another became general, it would do much to spread the knowledge of helpful experiments, and would make for a better international understanding, for as each settlement has a greater or larger sphere of influence among people of various classes, they are in a position to counteract the prevailing prejudice against the foreigner which, despite all the efforts of international socialism and labour in the international, is as strong among working men as among any other class of the community. The travel societies promoted in some of the Settlements for members of their clubs serve a similar purpose.

WOMEN'S SETTLEMENTS

Settlements for women are now as numerous as those for men, although the movement started a little later, and several men's Settlements have subsequently felt the necessity of the co-operation of women and have started a women's house. The work of men's and women's Settlements does not differ in essentials, but the method of approach is in the one case through the boys and the men, in the other through the girls and the women, and the best results are obtained through close touch being kept between the two. The women's Settlement is generally better supplied with whole time workers, as the men are more frequently engaged in earning their livings during the day. There is much work that can be best done in the daytime and by women, especially visiting the homes and all work in connection with women and young children. Secretarial work also is largely performed by women. It is important that whatever work is being done in a district should be extended to both sexes, otherwise there is a possibility of one-sided development. I have heard of a girls' club that did excellent work among a rather rough class of girls, with the result that the boys did not come up to their standard when the time came for them to marry.

There are also more paid posts for women than men, and the Settlement offers an alternative to a lonely life in lodgings, and also relieves the worker of domestic cares for which she is apt to have very little time, if engaged on paid social work.

THE SCHOOL MISSION

Most of the great public schools support missions or clubs in poor districts, and supply the funds and personnel necessary for their operation.

In some cases a parson is placed at the head, and the mission develops into a parish, in others the whole of the work is carried on by laymen, and there is sometimes no salaried head at all. In both cases the aim is to bring home to the boys at the school the claims on them that their poorer brothers have, and to influence not only the people of the district in which the mission or club is situated, but also the members and old members of the institution supporting it. The principal interest of the mission is generally a boys' club or several clubs, as it is considered that this is most likely to enlist the support of the school. The club boys will visit the school and play football there, or take part in shooting matches, etc., and senior boys from the school will entertain them, while boys from the school will assist in running the summer camp. The idea is that the mission should be supported by a continuous stream of voluntary workers composed of the old boys of the school, so that the school's support should be not merely pecuniary but personal.

This is the theory, but it is not always carried out in practice. The interest of the school is often very languid, and limited to a terminal subscription, an occasional chapel collection accompanied perhaps by a short burst of enthusiasm created by an eloquent sermon; for the rest the Mission is carried on by a parson, generally an old boy, and one or two voluntary helpers, but the sum total of its effect on the school is trifling.

This is unfortunate, as there are few institutions so entirely ignorant of and detached from the social problems that are to-day being discussed in the country generally as the public schools. With a few exceptions public school masters are very ignorant of matters outside their own work, and the rather narrow round of school interests and the curriculum excludes any study of the present-day problem.

History is often much neglected, and is generally somewhat antiquarian; economics and political science are not touched, and beyond the daily newspaper and the school debating society there is little to call the attention of the boys to the facts of industrial and social life.

It is not, of course, contended that social science

should take the place of any of the regular school subjects, for the whole school, but it is urged that for boys of 18 and 19 to leave a public school with practically no knowledge of social problems is something of a disgrace to the public school system. The training in political science of the average public school might be expressed by parodying Kipling—" What do they know of England who only the Empire know ? " The school mission gives an opportunity for interesting boys while still at school in social questions, but all depends on how the school mission is utilised. I have heard a headmaster declare that all that was really necessary was to give the boys a sentimental interest in the poor. While views such as this are current, little will be accomplished.

One thing that militates against the school mission is its ecclesiastical character, for the average healthy boy is not very interested in religious services or religious missions, and I am inclined to think that those undertakings that are entirely carried on by laymen wherein the religious objective is not stressed are more successful.

If the older boys from the school can come down to see the boys' club during the term and have a talk with those who are managing it, they are likely to retain a certain amount of interest, and if a boy visits it once or twice he will soon begin to find out that there is a good deal that he can do there, and that there is plenty he can learn. Work in a boys' club is one of the easiest ways of obtaining an introduction to social questions. Take the case of a boy from a public school knowing little or nothing of social and industrial matters, who decides, perhaps, at the invitation of a friend or from loyalty to his old school that runs a mission, or to the instinct for service that exists in everyone to assist in running a boys' club. At first he will be shy, then on getting to know the club boys he will find himself with a new outlook and shedding old prejudices. The rather noisy crowd of boys on bicycles with long quiffs of hair turned over the peaks of their caps, whom he always regarded as bounders, become human beings to him, and he appreciates their high spirits, and overlooks what he would formerly have called vulgarity. He goes out to referee for them at football, and finds that the only available ground is four miles away and he remembers that somewhere he had heard of an agitation for open spaces, while the question of getting them makes him consider transport problems, trains, rail and buses, and he may begin to enquire who is responsible for these services.

He finds his boys get there so late that the moon is already getting up, and perhaps his centre-forward, on whom he was relying, cannot get there at all; he finds it is a case of overtime, and the demand for shorter hours of labour becomes a reality; he has always played in the afternoon at school, and even when at work in town gets off in fairly good time; he realises now the value of a 48-hour week.

A little later he will perhaps visit one of his boys who is sick and begin to see the housing problem from the inside—perhaps the family cannot afford proper treatment for the boy, and he is forced to consider the provision now made for the sick, and further the wages question begins to interest him after he has had a talk with the boy's father, who is in the building trade and gets only occasional work.

In a year or two the thoughtless schoolboy will have

become interested in social problems in the concrete, and from this it is but a step to studying them in the abstract, and he soon sees how little his efforts can accomplish, and will perceive that the faults he sees are only the effects of greater causes.

The school club or mission should be run mainly as a means of educating the school in the idea of social service. If the school were to provide an adequate library of social and economic works, not only would the boy who has some experience of the school mission be likely to read them in order to find out more about the problem he has encountered there, but the boys who had read them would be likely to visit the mission to check their reading.

Even if no such teaching could be included in the curriculum yet it would be possible for a keen master to start a society like those devoted to natural history, art, etc., where those who were interested could discuss these subjects. It may be claimed that these subjects are out of place in school life, and could be better left till the boy goes to the University. But it must be remembered that comparatively few boys go to the University, and that 18 or 19 is an age when their working-class brothers have been earning their living for some years, and are frequently hard at work studying these very subjects.

THE FUTURE OF SETTLEMENTS

It is obviously difficult to prophesy as to the future of any particular piece of social machinery. At a time of changing ideas and big movements one cannot tell what adjustments may be necessary, but it is worth while here considering how far the settlements have fulfilled the ideas of their founders and what tendencies are discernible among those engaged in settlement work.

In the first place, the very name 'Settlement' suggests that, at the period when they were started, the lives of the working classes were something apart from those of the rest of the nation, so far apart, indeed, that to visit them was like entering a foreign and possibly savage territory where a fort was to be erected, from which expeditions could be sent to get in touch with the natives.

At the time the first settlement was formed there was some excuse for this idea, for conditions, say in East London, were far rougher than they are to-day, and it took a good deal of courage to live in a poor district. That is all changed to-day. East London is as safe to walk about in as most places, friendly relations have been established with the natives, and the settlers have found that the differences between classes are not as great as they thought. Thus an extension has taken place, and many people who would formerly have lived in settlements begin to find them unsatisfactory, and migrate into the district and take ordinary houses. In fact colonies are taking the place of settlements.

There is a certain artificiality about settlement life. However desirous people may be to get in touch with people of other classes it is not possible to do so thoroughly while living in a settlement. Of a necessity the rooms of the residents are partly used in common, and it is difficult to bring in working class friends to dinner or tea with the other residents. Further, settlements are for the bachelor and spinster for the most part, and if the social worker marries and wants to continue his or her work, he must move from the settlement; hence of recent years in a good number of cases we have people settling down and living in working-class districts, although their professional or business work may be in some other neighbourhood.

I think on the whole that this is a hopeful movement; we want to break up the huge collection of people of one class living in a special district, and return to a more natural system, and this is one of the ways whereby it can be done.

I think in the future the settlement will be, in the main, a place of training for social workers, and that outside of it will be families living in the district, many of them former residents who will have gained their interest in the district and in social work from the settlement, and will keep in touch with it, but will be essentially ordinary residents of the locality.

In a sense the settlements may be said to have done their work. Members of different classes do now know each other to a far greater extent than before.

The increase in the numbers of working men and, to a less extent, of working women who have had more than the education of the elementary school, who read, study and think for themselves has been very great, and the settlement worker is now far more only a partner and counsellor to the workers, than one who has superior knowledge and is out to 'uplift the working classes.'

I think then that the true function of settlements to-day comes under three heads:

First, as centres of all kinds of voluntary work for the good of a district, where workers and thinkers of all classes can meet freely and discuss their common problems, and where information and advice is always forthcoming.

Second, as places of training for young workers, where first-hand experience can be obtained, and to which people who like a communal life for part of their lives can go.

Third, as social laboratories, where new ideas can be worked out and experiments tried of every variety of new social effort.

A settlement must, it appears to me, move with the times, and those that merely carry on the old work that was applicable to earlier days are not being as useful as they might. A settlement to-day must be in closer touch than ever with the best minds of the working people of the district. It must be free from any taint of what is often described as charity-mongering and of any idea of superiority. It would be well if it could be supported and controlled by the people of the district, and get away entirely from the idea that it was supported by charitably disposed persons from outside. It would, I think, be well to drop the term 'Mission' altogether. A friend of mine who ran a club for years that was supported by a School always refused to say he ran a mission, for he held that if it was a case of mission, the supporters needed one quite as badly as the recipients of their bounty.

As has been stated above, social work is not the monopoly of any one class to-day, nor are social ideas, and the settlement of the future will be successful only in as far as it realises the fact that every class has its contribution to make to social science. The settlement of the future should, to my mind, cease to be an artificial growth planted by someone from outside, and become instead an integral part of the neighbourhood.

The conclusions on the settlement movement of an

acute foreign observer, Dr. Werner Picht, may be given here :

"It represents the noblest and most deeply humane attempt at the solution of the social problem. It has done great things in the service of love and knowledge, more than a well-thought-out logical irreproachable system of social work could have done. But it rests on the mistaken idea that a number of well-meaning cultured people could become neighbours to the poor whenever they chose. This is possible so long as they are carried over all hindrances by a wave of enthusiasm, or so far as their life is filled with living Christianity; for both can overcome all human obstacles, and it is there that the difficulty lies. The history of the movement shows that the task in itself is not unsolvable. Human bonds can be forged between men and women of different classes to the great profit of both sides. Here are settlements which carry into practice the neighbourhood idea in an ideal manner, and do a work which lies entirely outside the possibilities of an organisation. But this assumes a degree of latent human warmth combined with a tact and perseverance, such as in the long run the ordinary man has not at his disposal.

"The settlement places before the average man a heroic task and, by veiling it, makes it acceptable to him. Thus out of social idealism it was possible for a wide-reaching movement to be born which gained many forces that would otherwise have been lost to it and won for itself supporters in large circles. But it appears condemned, in its original shape, to suffer shipwreck on its own ideals, the severity of which it did not recognise."

LIST OF THE PRINCIPAL SETTLEMENTS

London

Bermondsey Settlement, Farncombe Street, Jamaica Road, S.E. Wesleyan. Women's Settlement, 149 Lower Road, Rotherhithe.

Cambridge House, 131 Camberwell Road, S.E. Church of England.

Canning Town Women's Settlement, Cumberland Road, Plaistow, E.

Catholic Settlement, Bermondsey, 8 Grange Road, Bermondsey.

Gonville and Caius Mission and Settlement, Battersea.

Haileybury House, Durham Row, Stepney.

Lady Margaret Hall Settlement, 129 Kennington Road, S.E.,

Mansfield House University Settlement, 89 Barking Road, E.

Maurice Hostel (men), 64 Britannia Street, Hoxton (women), 51 Herbert Street, Hoxton. Christian Social Union.

Oxford House, Bethnal Green, E. Church of England.

Oxford and Bermondsey Mission, Riley Street, Bermondsey, S.E.

Passmore Edwards Settlement, Tavistock Place, W.C.

Women's Presbyterian Settlement, 56 East India Dock Road, E.

The Ratcliff Settlement, London Street, Commercial Road, E.

Robert Browning Settlement, York Street, Walworth Road.

Rugby House, 292 Lancaster Road, Notting Hill, W.

St. Anthony's Settlement, Poplar. Catholic.

St. Cecilia's House Settlement, 531 Commercial Road, E. Catholic.

St. Helen's House, 91 The Grove, Stratford.

St. Hilda's East (Cheltenham Ladies' College Guild Settlement), 3 Old Nichol Street, Bethnal Green.

St. Margaret's House, 21 Old Ford Road, Bethnal Green, E. Church of England.

St. Mildred's House, Millwall, Isle of Dogs, Poplar, E.

St. Patrick's Club, Pier Head, Wapping. Catholic.

Toynbee Hall, 28 Commercial Street, Whitechapel.

Trinity Settlement, 60 Romford Road, Stratford.

United Girls' School Settlement, 19 Peckham Road, Camberwell.

Wellington College Mission, 179 East Street, Walworth.

Women's University Settlement, 44 Nelson Square, Blackfriars Road, S.E.

Provincial

Bath Citizen House, Chandos Buildings.

Birmingham Women's Settlement, 318 Summer Lane, Birmingham.

Bristol, The Broad Plain House, Broad Plain, Bristol. Congregational. The University Settlement, Barton Hill, Bristol.

Chesterfield Women's Settlement, Church Lane, Chesterfield, Derbyshire.

Ipswich Social Settlement, 133 Fore Street, Ipswich, Suffolk.

Leeds, The Red House Settlement, East Street, Leeds. Church of England.

Liverpool University Settlement, Nile Street, Liverpool. Victoria Women's Settlement, 294 Netherfield Road, Liverpool.

Manchester Art Museum and University Settlement, Ancoats Hall, Every Street, Manchester.

Middlesborough Congregational Women's Settlement, 132 Newport Road, Middlesborough.

Stoke-on-Trent Women's Settlement, Fenton House, Stoke-on-Trent.

Dundee Grey Lodge Women's Settlement.

Edinburgh New College Settlement, 48 Pleasance, Edinburgh. University Settlement, Surgeon Square, Infirmary Street, Edinburgh.

Glasgow Queen Margaret Settlement, 77 Port Street, Anderston, Glasgow.

Glasgow University Students' Settlement, 10 Possil Road, Garscube Cross, Glasgow.

Belfast Women Workers' Settlement, 55 Cumlin Road, Belfast.

The University Settlement in Cardiff, Walker Road, East Moors, Cardiff.

CHAPTER VIII

VARIETIES OF SOCIAL WORKERS

In this chapter some of the different activities of social workers will be considered, and some of the different types of worker that play their parts in social service. There is always the danger of considering that one's own special branch is all-important, and neglecting the efforts of others. The town dweller neglects the problems of the countryside, and the employer and the working man fail to see the relevance of each other's social activities.

Again, one is always inclined to depreciate the work that is done by those who take a different view of things from oneself, and the enthusiast for municipal or State organisation is apt to fail to allow credit to those who work for voluntary societies. It is probable that the present author has not, despite his endeavours to do so, avoided this pitfall.

Social service is inclusive, not exclusive, and a consideration of some of the various types of worker and how they co-operate to a common end despite themselves may help to drive home this point.

THE SOCIAL WORKER AS PIONEER

Perhaps the most important task of the social worker is to act as a pioneer in discovering new social groupings and new methods of advance. The social theorist may decide on grounds of general principle that this or that arrangement is good or bad for the society of his time, the social reformer or the revolutionary may advocate changes and may create a new public opinion, but it is, in the main, to the social worker that they must look for practical experiment and for the collection of data on which action can be taken. Thus a man may advocate copartnership on grounds of general principle, but it is only when the practical social worker, in this instance the enlightened employer, has actually put it into practice, that the possibilities and disadvantages of the scheme are made to appear.

Again all can dream of better houses and of garden cities, but it is to those who take the actual steps in building houses or planning garden cities and actually laying them out, that we are indebted for advances. This seems to me to be the real work to-day of those who adventure in social service—and it is largely the way in which social reform has been brought about in this country. First the individual has sought out a new method and proved its practicability, and then society has followed and adopted a new principle, or extended a service tentatively applied on a small scale to whole classes of the community or areas of the country. Each group of social workers, each Settlement has been a laboratory of social science in which new theories are tested, or applications adapted to this country of reforms initiated in foreign countries or overseas possessions.

In the sphere of housing and town planning in particular much has been done by the individual. As long ago as the sixties the work of Miss Octavia Hill and her friends demonstrated how much could be done by a system of rent-collecting by social workers to effect the reform of slum-areas, setting up a means whereby the urban landlord, who wished to regard his property from the point of view of the good of the tenants and not merely as a source of revenue, could obtain the assistance of a band of social workers to take the place of the mere agent for the collection of money.

Since that time the extension of municipal housing has been accompanied by the careful selection of tenants and still more of caretakers, whose business is not merely the condition of the buildings, but the promotion of ideas of good tenantry on the part of the inhabitants. It is sometimes considered that this form of work partakes too much of the interfering and grandmotherly quality, and that it does not contribute much to the solution of the housing question, but it has its place in housing reform for this reason.

When a slum area is cleared and new houses are built it is very seldom that the displaced persons return to the area and occupy the new houses, they generally drift off to some other district and form a new slum there, because they have lost the habits that make for good tenantry.

While it is true that there are many factors that make the slum, such as bad buildings and low wages, and while most people now agree that it is the sty that makes the pig, not the pig that makes the sty, yet there exists a residue of people who will make a slum of the best houses, and for these some method such as that initiated by Miss Hill is necessary.

The enthusiastic social reformer is sometimes apt to rely too much on bettering environment and not enough on bettering the individual, and rent-collecting schemes are of value as setting up a better standard in a slum area and thus influencing the whole neighbourhood.

The old pride in the city as a place of beauty and not merely a number of houses giving shelter and little else has been reinforced by the garden city movement and the new insistence on housing and town planning. It is depressing to consider how, during the period of the growth of population, and the emergence of the big centres of population in this country, the idea of town planning was entirely absent, so that our housing problems are the result of the neglect and lack of civic ideals of our immediate ancestors. Even to-day when the question has had a considerable history in social reform movements, and when there is a fairly large public educated in ideas of citizenship, discussion is still carried on too often in the terms of working class dwellings rather than homes for the people.

Despite the Housing and Town Planning Act, there are still local authorities that think only of erecting an adequate number of dwellings instead of considering how they can extend their city to the best advantage of the community, and how to build cities that shall make a good life, and not a mere existence, possible.

That some progress has been made is due in the main to the social experimenters. Messrs. Cadbury and Lord Leverhulme have shown how an industrial area can be laid out so that the houses are beautifully grouped, pleasant to the eye and diversified with open spaces, but Cadburys and Levers are the exception. Since their pioneer efforts a good many experiments have been made, to two of which reference must be made.

The Hampstead Garden Suburb, which owes its

origin to Mrs. Barnett, calls for notice not only on account of its town-planning and beautiful houses, but as a social experiment in which an attempt is made to get away from the modern custom of segregating the population into groups, middle class suburbs, working class districts or suburban areas. The idea is to combine in one area provision for all classes, so as to effect in the realm of town-planning that union of classes aimed at by Canon Barnett in the settlement movement; in fact, to counteract the tendency for society to split into horizontal groups. Further, it endeavours to create not a mere suburb, but an organism with a life of its own; the typical suburb is the negation of civic life, a mere mass of houses without a real centre, and with little to give a common interest to its inhabitants. No one ever boasts of being an Acton man or a Willesden woman, and the Hampstead experiment is the attempt to create a new kind of suburb where the inhabitants shall feel themselves citizens and not merely occupiers of dormitories.

The other more ambitious experiment is the Letchworth garden city, where an entirely new city has been created with its own industries. This seems to me an enormous advance on the usual housing scheme, because of its recognition of the need of a new kind of city where the town is in the country and the country in the town.

The overgrowth of towns increases the difficulties of local government enormously, for their great size prevents each citizen from taking an active part in communal affairs and cuts at the root of democratic government based on locality.

The success of the Letchworth experiment suggests that, at the present crisis in housing, it might be better to conduct a survey of the great urban centres, and see whether there are not industries that might be carried on just as well in some less crowded part of the country, so that instead of adding ring after ring to a city like London and thus creating an ever growing congestion at the centre, it would be possible to remove certain industries with the population dependent on them away from London altogether.

In chapter two it has been shown how charities that at one time made the sole provision for classes such as the sick and the aged have been gradually superseded by extensions of the functions of central and local governing authorities, and that their main work is to work in with the state authorities supplying certain services, particularly those of the nature of personal influence, that can better be performed through voluntary societies. None the less, although charity is ceasing to be in the main a voluntary ambulance service to the community, it must be pointed out that it is voluntary effort that has paved the way, and that but for voluntary effort many of these services would not have been initiated. The development of a school medical service owes much to voluntary experiment, particularly to the clinic at Deptford carried on by Miss Margaret Macmillan, provision for birth and infancy, starting schools for mothers, pure milk depots and meetings of parents for advice and discussion, such as those carried on under the auspices of the mothers' union, were all worked out by voluntary workers.

THE SOCIAL WORKER IN THE COUNTRY

The greater part of the literature of social service deals with the problems of the towns, and the equally unsatisfactory conditions in rural areas are apt to be neglected. There are several reasons for this; first, because for many years the ambition was to make England the workshop of the world and the supply of cheap food from overseas seemed to be so secure that little attention was bestowed on the state of agriculture; those who really understood the conditions of rural life were for the most part people who were wedded to old ideas and looked backwards rather than forwards, while the reformers were generally town dwellers whose enthusiasm for abstract principles was not equalled by their knowledge. Secondly, there was no strong and articulate demand from the workers themselves. Since the collapse of Joseph Arch's movement in the seventies and the emigration of many of the most active agricultural labourers overseas, the trade union lingered on only in Norfolk, and the co-operative distributive movement never really took root in the villages of purely agricultural districts. Thirdly, while the closest investigation has been applied to urban areas and a multitude of accurate studies produced, till recently those dealing with rural areas were less complete and were generally produced more with a view of supporting political propaganda than in the spirit of scientific research. Fourthly, rural conditions being scattered over a wide area do not make such an appeal to the sympathies of the observer as the masses of poverty visible in the towns. Rural housing evils scattered throughout a thousand villages and masked very often by picturesque thatch and ivy fail to make the same impression as the stark ugliness and filth of East or South London, or Salford and Wigan.

To-day there is a change. The war has brought

home to us the ultimate dependence of the town on the country. The need for home grown food has drawn attention to the lack of system in our rural life. The need of a more scientific organisation of agriculture so as to take advantage of the methods applied to other industries and so increase production was demonstrated during the war, and the extent to which small plots of ground could be utilised, suggests that there is great scope for co-operation on the part of a number of workers each producing on a small scale.

The organisation of agricultural labourers which was just beginning to revive in the years before the war has suddenly taken immense strides forward. In counties such as Berkshire and Oxfordshire, formerly considered practically dead from the trade union point of view, almost every agricultural worker is now in union. Further a large number of town people have worked on the land during the war, either on farms or on allotments, and the agricultural worker has been brought into close contact with his fellows from the towns, so that there is a flood of new ideas penetrating the country.

Here then is a field ripe for new social experiment where the application of the social service spirit is needed to recreate rural life.

Local government in the country has not been so progressive as in the towns. Here and there a keen education committee has done excellent work, and three or four of the counties have really put the Small Holdings Act into force, but despite the good work done here and there, on the whole there is not very much enterprise. Where things have been done at all it has been generally due to the energy of one or two individuals. Here and there a parish council has worked to make the village more attractive, and has taken advantage of its powers, thus becoming a really effective force in local life, but this is exceptional.

There is plenty of work then for the local administrator: the new education act, providing for continuation schools calls for very skilful adaptation to the needs of rural districts both in contriving where and how classes shall be held, and of what type the education given is to be. The Ministry of Health Act and the measures that will follow it call for careful consideration as to the best unit of administration in rural areas for combining effectively the provision made in the county area for the prevention and cure of disease, and the ensuring of central control and local automomy.

The rural housing question, acute before the war, is now critical. Valuable experiments have been made as to the best form of cottage but with a tendency to go for cheapness before everything. The fact that the demand for houses is great at the moment ought not to blind people to the fact that what is needed is not just bare accommodation, but, that unless houses fit for people to live and bring up families in, are provided, all talk of "back to the land" is useless. This mistake has been made in the towns by erecting blocks of working class dwellings which although they may be well built are not what the people want. It must be realised that if the cost of building materials and labour have gone up during the war, so has the standard of life, and that workers demand that elementary conveniences such as a bath should be provided.

It is now some years since the "back to the land" cry was started, but not very much has been done to resettle the country.

It would seem that what is really needed is a full consideration of what is the best form of economic organisation for each part of the country, for without this it is useless to try and get the town worker to return to the village. The experiments in training carried on in their farm colonies by the Salvation Army and by the Central Unemployed Body for London in the Hollesley Bay experiment has shown that it is possible to train the man from the towns, but the difficulty has always been to fit him into rural life when trained. Mr. Joseph Fels' colony of small holders, despite its failure to attain success, was a useful experiment on a small scale. Judging from the example of Ireland, the co-operative system seems to offer the greatest possibilities for the future, and the social worker who lives in the country could usefully assist agencies such as the Agricultural Organisation Society in spreading the principles of co-operation and helping to guide new societies. Above all there is need for brightening rural life. The complaint of the average town worker who goes back to the land is that his life is so dull. It is not that he pines for cinemas and crowded streets, but that there is not enough life, not enough sociability. A movement that is making considerable strides is that for forming village councils, especially for the women, in order to formulate and put into practice new ideas.

THE SOCIAL INVESTIGATOR

A particular form of social work is that of social investigation. It is not always realised in passing criticisms upon our predecessors how small was the store of knowledge upon which they had to work, how little systematised were such data as were available, and how widespread was the ignorance, not merely of the relationship of cause and effect in the problems which charitable workers set out to remedy, but of the ideas and aspirations of those whom it was sought to help, whereas all social workers to-day have a great store of information resulting from experience and investigation of others, whereby they can guide their actions, and all must acknowledge the great debt owed to the numbers of people who have devoted their time and money to a scientific investigation into general or particular problems of society.

Every person engaged in social work has the opportunity of repaying some of this debt and assisting others, by putting his or her experiences into the common stock, and thus adding to the general collection of observed facts upon which action can be taken. It is not possible for the ordinary rank and file of social worker to hope to rival skilled investigators, but each one can take his part by cultivating habits of careful observation and analysis of the pieces of social machinery that come under his notice. There is one particular kind of work which is well within the power of every social worker, and this is the watching of the effect of different pieces of social legislation. Some general act of parliament is passed and many are content to imagine that the subject is then finished with, the specific evil has been provided for and they think that they can turn to something else. All legislation is experimental and it is necessary to watch it in the working to see if the effects of any particular act are those that have been anticipated by its author, or whether some other factors have come in that will neutralise its advantages: one has to consider not only its practical effect on material things, but its psychological results on the lives and characters of the portion of society affected by it.

Further, it is one thing to enact legislation, it is another to get it carried out. The work of even the best inspectors needs to be supplemented by the constant vigilance of voluntary workers. Modern acts of parliament are very puzzling to the layman. The skilled draughtsman or lawyer can understand them at a glance, but to-day their provisions have to be known and acted upon by a large number of people little skilled in studying legal documents, and an immense amount of irritation is caused by the attempts of the uninstructed to find out just what it is they are supposed to do.

Take, for instance, the National Health Insurance Act, whereby some fourteen million people had to take definite steps to enrol themselves in Societies: it was found necessary in this case to enrol a special corps of official explainers to go about the country expounding its provisions to the people; this was a good precedent, but it has not been followed up to the same extent when other pieces of social legislation have been passed, and it is part of the duty of the social worker, and a very valuable duty, to make himself master of the contents of recent social legislation, so as to be ready not only to answer any questions that may be put to him, but to take active steps to inform those for whom he is working of the way in which they are affected by these enactments. The successful working of any piece of social legislation depends on keeping up the goodwill which caused it to be passed, and this goodwill is apt to disappear in the number of minor vexations incidental to putting its provisions into practice.

Another instance where it was found necessary by social workers to conduct investigations to find out the results of legislation, was that of the Trades Boards Act. Minimum wages were established in the tailoring trade, but it was necessary to see whether in fact the workers, especially the outworkers, were getting the rates laid down by the Board, and to see what effect the Act was having on the organisation of the industry, whether work was being driven into the factory or concentrated into the hands of a few large firms, and what was the effect on the poorest workers, in fact to find out what were the social results of the measure. Results of investigations of this kind have been made public in Mr. Tawney's books on the minimum rates in the tailoring trade and in the chain-making trade, and a similar work was performed by Miss Bulkeley in examining the administration and effects of the feeding of school children by public authorities. These investigations would not have been possible without the co-operation of a number of social workers who were closely acquainted with the districts most affected by those Acts, and who had the confidence of the workers in those industries.

There is then much work to be done by those engaged in social service in investigation, and this can best be done by a number of workers in collaboration with some one of experience at their head to collate their efforts; but besides the collection of information there is urgent need for systematised thought on social subjects. Meetings of social workers are too often occasions on which details of practical organisation are worked out, and not enough attention is given to the consideration of theory. Theory and practice must work together, it is no good to leave theory to the universities and practice to the social workers. This avoidance of theoretical discussion may be due to the fear of causing dissension among the practical workers, but it is regrettable, especially at a time when all kinds of changes are taking place.

A subject, for instance, on which valuable work might be done is that of the proper sphere of the family, the group and the State in domestic life. The feeding of school children was adopted not so much on the theory that it was best that children should be fed at school, but from the fact that education and the children themselves were suffering from children going to school improperly fed. Discussion of the subject was largely on the question of whether it would lead to pauperism or not, whereas what is wanted is the consideration of whether the school meal is a special contrivance for the benefit of the very poor or a beginning of communal meals. During the war the communal kitchen has come into being, and the whole question of whether all meals should be taken in the home or some outside is ripe for discussion : it is a complicated question of social habit and convenience, and is not to be dismissed by phrases like breaking up the family. Again the question of the organisation of the home, so as to relieve the mother of some of the excessive strain that she now undergoes in poor families is worth investigation, the institution of créches so as to give some relief from incessant care of small children, the question as to how far arrangements could be made for common baths and washhouses for a group of families, or common kitchens, is ripe for experiment. In few departments of life has less thought been applied to scientific management than the home, and a group of workers might well try experiments in conjunction with working class mothers to find out what improvements can be made, and how they would be likely to be received. Meanwhile we continue to build houses on the lines of the self-contained family, which we have inherited from rural conditions.

Again, workers for charitable societies might well consider the proper delimitation of function between charity and the State in any particular field of work in which they may be interested. As a rule the person interested in charity is apt to be jealous of the interference of any other agency into his or her own particular field, but as, from time to time, extensions of State interference come about, it should be the task of those engaged in any charities to see how they can utilise the interests that support their charity in some other work or how best they can co-operate. Above all, the social worker should be constantly on the lookout for new needs.

To turn to the social work of the investigator proper, we may consider first of all the district survey initiated by the investigations into the conditions of life, labour, religious and social influences in East London made by Charles Booth and his collaborators between the years 1881 and 1893. The work is impressive, not only from its vast size but from the fact that it was practically the first attempt to deal in detail with the whole life of a very large area, examining on the spot the actual condition of the inhabitants and the effect of social and industrial causes. It is difficult to overestimate its effect on the opinions of the general public and of social workers in particular. For the first time a careful and impartial survey of conditions in a poor district was made and the discovery that at least 30 per cent. of the population were living below the poverty line, an estimate borne out by the subsequent enquiry of Mr. Rowntree into conditions at York, dispelled for ever the complacent assumption that the bulk of the people were able to keep themselves in tolerable comfort, and the poverty was mainly due to the moral deficiencies of individuals. This system of investigation has since been followed up by others. Mr. Hawkins' "Norwich," Miss Jebb's "Cambridge," and Messrs. Bowley and Burnett Hursts' "Livelihood and Poverty" have applied similar methods to provincial towns, while rural conditions have been dealt with in a similar way in the study of Corsley, by the late Miss Maud Davies, and by Mr. Mann in his investigation of "Ridgmount." This method of district survey has been undertaken also by many groups of Settlement workers in the United States. Much useful work of this nature has been performed by Government departments, such as the comparative studies of conditions of life, wages, prices and hours of labour in various countries, published by the Board of Trade, and the masses of evidence produced for the use of the Commission on the Poor Laws. More recently the publications on studies of industrial fatigue among munition workers has contributed very much to a realisation of what modern industrial life is really like, and as to the effect of these material conditions on the social life of the nation.

A good example of a piece of investigation by a social worker on a specific subject is Sir William Beveridge's study of unemployment worked out while he was a resident at Toynbee Hall which was one of the causes for the adoption of the system of Labour Exchanges in this country. It may be contrasted as a piece of social work with the numerous funds got up by the Press for the unemployed in East London during years of distress. Canon Barnett described their effects at the time as increasing poverty by making it a domestic asset, degrading the poor and hardening the common conscience by raising the standard of sensation required to elicit charity. The contrast is clear between a piece of work which investigated causes and suggested preventives, and a work which only dealt with symptoms and worked by immediate and temporary palliatives. This is not to deny the necessity of agitation in order to create the necessary feeling for the forcing on of reforms, but to show that the social worker must take up the task of investigation so that forces of enthusiasm may not be dissipated by being applied to faulty machinery.

It is impossible here to deal at any length with the work of the numbers of investigators who have in the past or in the present so powerfully contributed to social reform. An exception may perhaps be made by referring to the voluminous works of Mr. and Mrs. Sidney Webb whose investigations into local governments, education and industrial organisations among other subjects, have laid all social workers under a heavy debt. The strongest opponents of Fabianism, whether they belong to the old individualist school with its opposition to all extensions of State activity, or are anti-bureaucratic advocates of control of their lives by the workers themselves, have to work on the basis of the investigations of these two untiring social workers. The difficulty of the social worker to-day is not so much the lack of information as the difficulty of keeping touch with the flood of publications covering every part of the field of social science. The student is confronted not only with the conclusions of those engaged in charitable work, and the mass of statistics produced by Government departments, but with investigations made from every point of view, from that of the economist, the physical scientist, the moral philosopher, and the theorist in political science and sociology. All of these are engaged in social service, and investigation into the forms of thought of human beings and the philosophy of social development is quite as much needed as into the practical details and machinery of social life.

THE SOCIAL WORKER AS AGITATOR

Every social worker is almost certain to be also an agitator. If he or she learns certain facts and believes that they are due to certain causes which are beyond the power of an individual to remove, it is impossible to rest contented with the limited amount of good that can be done by following old methods and agitation to get people to see a new point of view. The word 'agitator' is distasteful to many, it calls up a picture of a person who is rather unbalanced, honest perhaps, but wrong headed, possibly dishonest, troubling the waters with a view to fishing in them for his own benefit. This is mainly the point of view of the person who is on the whole contented with things as they are, whose general attitude is that of Lord Melbourne—"Why can't you let it alone?" Nevertheless the agitator has a most important part to play in social progress, and the social worker owes him a big debt. The agitator of one age is recognised by the next as a prophet ; our fathers may have stoned him but we whiten his sepulchre; thus such men as Owen, Holyoake, Lovett, and Cobbett, were, in their day, agitators of the type that are frequently denounced in the public press, although on a quiet reading of their time and a realisation of the difficulties that they had to face, we recognise their single-mindedness and admire their courage. The great obstacle to all social reform is not so much the opposition of vested interests, though that is formidable enough, but the apathy of the general public, and it is the work of the agitator to keep stirring up the sluggish souls of ordinary men and women, and to present them in as powerful a manner as possible with one particular point of view.

The agitator then takes his place as a definite type of social worker, his particular function being to concentrate attention on particular aspects of the social problem, to spread information or at least a desire for information, and to generate the power necessary to make the slow moving machinery of society work. We may consider agitators as divided into three main types. There is first the man or woman who agitates for one particular piece of reform. Men such as Shaftesbury, Plimsoll, Howard, belong to this class. Their agitation is not related to general changes in Society, they attack particular abuses, and while from their singleness of purpose they get great driving force, they are apt to be narrow and one idead. A typical instance is the teetotal enthusiast, who gets so wrapped up in his propaganda that he attributes all social evils to the sale of intoxicating liquors;

another is the land nationaliser or single-taxer, of whom the best type is Henry George.

This type of agitator is frequently also a practical worker. He endeavours to carry out his ideals at the present time, and almost all social workers are to a greater or less extent of this type.

The second type is that of the scientifically-minded agitator. Such for instance was the group of men who founded the Fabian Society, whose agitation took the form of investigating facts, supplying other reformers with ammunition, and permeating the minds of the ruling classes. An example of an agitation for the adoption of a certain piece of social legislation, which was at the same time concerned with a propagation of particular views on the organisation of Society, was that for putting into effect the proposals of the minority report of the Poor Law. Such work as this is almost as much educational as propagandist. The attack is made rather on the mind than on the heart, the object being to supply practical methods of putting into effect the desires of less educated agitators. The third type is the agitator pure and simple. He may have, indeed generally has, views of a complete change of the basis of Society. He attacks the general social arrangements on every possible occasion, and any particular cause to which he attaches himself is considered only as a battle forming part of his general campaign. To this type belongs Robert Owen, for, although he was responsible for many practical experiments, and was the spiritual father of factory legislation, welfare work in factories, the co-operative movement, and to some extent the syndicalist and Guild Socialist movements of to-day, he was in the main concerned with the advocacy of a new form of Society that should be built up on his view of the importance of environment. To this type belong many labour agitators, of whom perhaps the finest type was the late James Keir Hardie. He was filled with the strongest possible sense of the injustice of present conditions of Society, and his heart was apt to rule his head. He would take up almost any unpopular cause of people whom he thought to be oppressed, whether they were Indians or Egyptians abroad, or working men or women at home. It is such men as he that create the driving force that is necessary before any reforms can be brought about, and although this type sometimes degenerates into mere futile abuse of existing institutions or attacks on individuals, yet in the main they offer a great example of self-denial and devotion to the cause that they take in hand. These three types are to be found combined in many persons, but the division can generally be made in accordance with the bias to one or other that any individual shows.

What then should be the attitude of the social worker towards agitation ? Should he be content to continue working at some particular piece of remedial work, or should he concern himself with reform movements ? The paid social worker is in a difficult position in this matter. Whatever his views may be, it is clear that he must not involve the organisation by which he is employed, and which may be supported by persons of very various views, in his own particular hobbies. But I would claim that so long as he does not do this he should be entitled to the full rights of a citizen. There is always the likelihood that he will be hampered by the fear of arousing unnecessary opposition or causing withdrawal of subscriptions and help from the organisation to which he is attached, if he is too outspoken in his advocacy of what may be thought to be extreme views. The social worker, however, must have definite views—must have formed some clear conception of what kind of society he wishes to see produced—and it is, I think, a mistake for him to hold aloof from reform movements. Whatever he does or does not do, his views will probably become known, and it is pandering to narrow-mindedness if from a fear of estranging others, he does not, upon suitable occasions, speak his mind. This is not to suggest that the social worker should be for ever, in season and out of season, thrusting his views down the throats of his co-workers, but simply to assert that in social service one must be ready to work with others of whose views one may not approve, and that the social worker has as much right to make clear his own outlook as anybody else.

A particular class of agitator is the writer, whether novelist, poet or dramatist. From the time of Dickens and Charles Reade to our own day there have always been authors who have combined the zeal of the social reformer with the skill of the story-teller and portrayer of character. Even to-day it is probable that to many people Dickens' picture of the workhouse is more vivid than the actual institution. Oliver Twist represents a past Poor Law system, but it is its faithful portrayal of the spirit of Poor Law administration that has fixed itself in the minds of all.

We have already mentioned Kingsley, and we may also recall George Eliot and Mrs. Gaskell as portrayers of the effects of the industrial revolution. In our own day we can recall the effect of such a book as Mr. Upton Sinclair's "Jungle," in calling attention to the particular abuses of the Chicago stock-yards, Mr. Norris' "Octopus," denouncing the railroad trusts, and Mr. Winston Churchill's "Coniston" and "The Inside of the Cup" as examples from America of the literature of exposure; while Mr. Galsworthy's "Strife," "The Silver Box" and "Justice," and Shaw's "Widowers' Houses" and "Mrs. Warren's Profession," among others, are instances of the use of the stage as an assistance to propaganda as well as being contributions to dramatic art.

The particular function of the literary agitator is to arouse interest in the large number of people who are unwilling, as a rule, to read a book with an avowedly serious purpose, but are lured into an interest in social matters almost unconsciously, accepting the pill in the jam. Thus many a man who would not read a book on sociology has read Mr. H. G. Wells' imaginative works and has gone on to read "New Worlds for Old" or "A Modern Utopia." These very few instances, which could be multiplied many times by examples from the literature of this and foreign countries, show how greatly the social problem forces itself into every kind of work. Perhaps one of the best ways of realising the changed outlook of to-day is to read not only the greatest masters of their time, who will in general be ahead of their age, but the ordinary rank and file of novelists. The assumptions made in the typical Victorian novel are very different from those of to-day: in the middle of last century the rich man needed no apology for his existence; nowadays there is a slight note of uneasiness, and if the hero is very rich, care will be taken to show what a good landlord or employer he is.

THE BUSINESS MAN AS A SOCIAL WORKER

What contribution can the business man, *qua* business man, make to social service ? The answer to this is best given by reference to some of the methods of social advance that have been worked out by employers of labour, some of them carrying on business in a small way, others among the leaders of the industrial world. It is not intended here to refer to the work of such men as Charles Booth and others whose social work was not directly connected with their business, but rather with the men who have sought out new methods of organisation in industry, or have applied themselves to a serious consideration of the conditions of work of their employees, or have rendered service in other ways to the solution of the problems of industrial life.

Let us name some of the difficulties that lie before the employer who endeavours to carry out social reform in his business. First he has to face the suspicion of his motives by those whom he wishes to benefit. The average worker is not unnaturally suspicious of his employer. In these days when the old personal relations subsisting between master and man have largely given place to impersonal relations between companies or trade organisations on the one hand, and trade unions acting through their officials on the other, when throughout industry employers and employed are divided into two camps, and war is frequent and peace only an armed neutrality, it is not easy to attempt to establish a different relationship ; to persuade the workers that there are interests in common between masters and men and that the motives for any action on the part of the employer are not directed by self-interest, but by a sincere desire for the betterment of the workers, and as a contribution to the solution of a social problem. This then is the first difficulty to get rid of, the atmosphere of suspicion, and establish cordial relations.

Secondly, there is the likelihood of the actions of the reforming employer being resented by others in the same trade. This is not necessarily due to any indifference to the welfare of their employees, or to mere stupidity and hostility to all change. In any trade there will be employers less well situated than others, or working on a small capital, or on a very narrow margin of profit, to whom the introduction of higher wages, shorter hours of labour, or better conditions in the works by the reforming employer may mean demands for similar reforms from their own men which they cannot afford, or at least think they cannot afford. The reforming employer is, as a rule, among the leaders in his trade, and able to make experiments, and perhaps able to afford to give better conditions than others. One of the principal services that the enlightened employer can render is the demonstration of the possibility of some demand or other for better conditions. Thus at a time when the bulk of employers declared for the necessity of child labour in the cotton mills and for the working of cruelly long hours, it was Robert Owen, a successful millowner, who demonstrated that a mill could be run profitably without this slavery of the young, and at a time when the current idea was that Satan was so exceedingly active among working people that it was in the interests of morality that children and adults should have as little time as possible between work and sleep, during which he could find work for idle hands to do, that Owen demonstrated the superior moral result of good conditions and education as counteractions to the Tempter.

Again, of later years agitations for a shorter working day and for increased earnings by working men have been met by arguments pointing out the dangers of under-cutting by foreign cheap labour, and alleging that high wages and short hours must inevitably lead to bankruptcy. These arguments have been controverted by economists pointing out the economy of high wages, that you could not get more out of a man than you put in, and demonstrating the loss incurred by working more than a certain number of hours, owing to the increase in accidents, spoiled work, etc. in the last hour, from industrial fatigue; but these counter arguments do not have half the effect on other employers as the demonstrations by such well-known captains of industry as Lord Leverhulme, who has actually put the matters in dispute to the test and demonstrated the practicability of the reform.

Employers as a whole are apt to have a deep distrust of the theorist, and to put their trust in the practical man. Employers also are in the main conservative, and each new provision, whether for shorter hours, abolition or restriction of child labour, or even for the fencing of machinery, is apt to be hailed as the last nail in the coffin of British industry, hence the value of the support of the enlightened employer. A recent case may be cited of the action of the well-known Lancashire firm of Tootal, Broadhurst & Lee, offering their strongest support to the abolition of the half-time system in the Lancashire cotton trade.

Again, the substitution of peaceful arbitration in industrial disputes for the method of the strike and the lock-out owes much to the far-sighted employers who, instead of taking up an attitude of blind hostility to trade unions and refusing them recognition, saw that the demand of the individual worker to negotiate with his employer through his union was reasonable, considering the disparity existing between the economic position of the single operative and his master, and recognised that to changed conditions of industry new methods must be applied. Among such may be mentioned men like Sir Rupert Kettle, who did so much to promote conciliatory methods. These men recognised that the time thus spent in sitting on boards and legislating for the trade was not time wasted, but was well worth while to secure contentment among their workers and peace in the industry.

A second great field of work for the employer is the introduction of better conditions in the factory and workshop. The study of the best conditions of lighting, heating and atmosphere, the provision of proper sanitary and washing apparatus, the provision of dining-rooms, where the workers can eat the meals they bring with them, or of canteens where good meals can be provided, are all matters in which some individual employer has led the way. The well-known Cadbury works at Bournville are important, not only for what they are, but for the higher standard that they have set up, and it may be noted here that it now pays a firm to advertise that they give good conditions, and to show photographs of their works with all the various provision made for the comfort of the workers, and that this should be so argues that the conception of the responsibility of the consumer for the conditions under which the commodities he uses are produced has been sufficiently accepted to make it worth the attention of employers from the business point of view.

There are those who would argue that none of these things partake of social service, insomuch as the employer ultimately benefits from the superior efficiency of his labour force. It may or may not be true of any particular instance that virtue in industrial matters is its own reward, but it is certain that the spirit in which those men pioneered these improvements has been one of a philanthropic nature, and that there are employers who are willing to take the risk of losses in order to do their duty to those who are in their service.

More recently, particular attention has been paid to questions of industrial fatigue and the conditions of working in modern industry, close observation having been brought to bear owing to the introduction of new classes of labour into munition work during the war, and the supervision of the whole group of amenities now known as industrial welfare is being entrusted to special officers known as Welfare Supervisors. Begun first with women and girls, and extended now to boys, and in some cases to men, this interesting development of industrial life is still to some extent on trial. The duty of the supervisor is to be the link between the management and the workers in all matters relating to welfare. As a rule this officer takes on all new labour, arranges with the co-operation of the workers for the control of canteens, games, or any other recreational activities that may be carried on in connection with the works, and is responsible for inquiring into cases of absence or bad time-keeping. He or she is in a position requiring considerable tact, for unless the confidence of the workers is obtained the work will be a failure, but on the other hand the welfare worker is the servant of the employer and paid by them. The terms Welfare and Welfare Worker or Supervisor are not very happy perhaps; they suggest rather old-fashioned paternalism, and perhaps emphasise too much the recreational and philanthropic side of the movement, and many employers dislike them. The word 'Welfare' does, however, at present hold the field in official publications. Perhaps a better term would be 'Works Co-ordination Officer,' expressing that the special function of the officer is to co-ordinate the management and the workers, and suggesting that he or she is a definite part of the normal staff of an up-to-date factory, rather than the exceptional hobby of a philanthropic employer.

The growing recognition of the importance of good conditions of labour and *esprit de corps* in the works, and their effects on the output and smooth running of the industrial machine, are vividly shown by the setting up of this specialised service in many businesses, and it may be pointed out that while the movement owes much to the encouragement of a Government department, it was first pioneered by private firms. The position offers a new profession, combining the interests of many forms of social work, and offers much scope to the right sort of person.

The divorce of the worker from all interest in his work and the need for finding some stimulus to effort beyond the mere danger of losing the situation if the work is not up to standard in quality and quantity, has led to many efforts being made to supply this want. More especially during the war period when labour was scarce and therefore at a premium has this need been felt. There is, too, a growing recognition on the part of many employers of the right of the worker to a greater control over his conditions of labour and a more direct share in the product of industry; this has led to many experiments in the direction of works committees and councils, formed on the lines recommended in the Whitley Report, and, both now and in the past, to attempts to devise some satisfactory form of copartnership or profit-sharing.

The copartnership and profit-sharing movement has not met with any great enthusiasm from the bulk of the workers in industry, and trade unions in particular have with a few exceptions been not merely lukewarm but hostile.

This is due in a large measure to the suspicion, which in some cases has been justified, that these were only devices to side-track the trade-union movement, cause division in the ranks, and get the worker to put out more energy for benefits that would prove illusory.

While some of its advocates have not been single-hearted in their advocacy, the majority are endeavouring to seek for a way of escape from the present system, which will unite the interests of master and man, and while seeing that labour has its share in the profits, leave scope for private enterprise and the reward of business ability.

It is not necessary here to examine the various forms of profit-sharing or copartnership, in some of which working men are associated in the management of the business, while in others they have the right to a share of the profits without participation in control; nor is it necessary to consider whether this form of organisation is suitable to modern industry or to speculate on the chances of the conversion of masters and men to its principles. Rather will it be noted as an instance of the kind of useful experiment in the organisation of industry that can be made by employers. At the present time the demand of labour for an increased share in the direction of the conditions under which the bulk of their waking day is spent, and even for the control of industry by the workers themselves, or at least a share in the control, gives a special interest to all experiments in this direction. While the copartnership movement provides in some cases for a share being granted to the operatives in the management of individual businesses, the new claim is rather for a share in the direction of whole industries considered as units, and is based at least in part on the claim that they should be carried on as services for the benefit of the community.

Whatever may be the view taken as to the desirability or possibility of any such new basis for industries, it will be all to the good if those who have the direction of industry experiment freely and thus provide the data for the future.

CHAPTER IX

THE SOCIAL SERVICE OF WORKING CLASSES

It has been pointed out above that it is necessary to give an extended range to the terms 'social worker' and 'social service.' The everyday meaning of social worker suggests someone from a superior social class who, through some religious or charitable motive, endeavours to assist the poor, but in this series it is given a wider meaning so as to include all those whose work is directly social in its motive and effects.

Voluntary social effort is not confined to any one class, nor do all movements of social advance come from above: many, and these not the least important, come as the expression of the aims of those who feel that their conditions of life need alteration; and without waiting for a lead from those in better circumstances, they endeavour to work out their own salvation, and in doing so produce new forms of social machinery. In this chapter the various social groupings of those whose means are in the main limited to their weekly earnings will be considered.

Associations of working men and women, whether as producers, consumers, mutual insurers, or fellow-citizens, have of late years been attracting increased attention, not merely from those who are immediately affected by their activities, such as the employing, professional and shopkeeping classes, but from the students of social and political science. They are seen not to be mere temporary groupings called into life to meet some special occasions, but natural organs of human society evolved to fulfil definite functions that cannot be undertaken by the individual in isolation. In their book " Industrial Democracy " Mr. and Mrs. Sidney Webb point out that it is remarkable how long it has taken our professors and leaders of thought to realise how great a reservoir of experiment in democratic government exists in the records and practice of the trade-union movement. University teachers in political science were still confining themselves to classic writers on theories of the democratic State, when beneath the surface these very theories were being put to the test. Discussions on the referendum might deal with Switzerland or the *plébiscite* of Napoleon III., but ignored the long-continued experiments of the Boilermakers' Society. Central Government and Local Autonomy might be illustrated from ancient history or colonial and foreign experience without a sign that the question was a burning one among the operatives by whose labours the theorists were clothed, fed and housed. To-day no theorist can afford to neglect the valuable lessons to be learnt from a study of the devices adopted by the great industrial democratic bodies to secure that the central control necessary to stable government and vigorous action should be combined with the fullest local autonomy and the subordination of the paid expert to the will of the majority whose servant he is.

There is a tendency in the minds of most men to over-simplify the problems with which they are faced and the phenomena they encounter which is particularly dangerous in social matters. Affairs to-day are so complex that it is hard to take into account all factors and to see all sides, so that most people see only the features that they wish to see. We look at a man only in relation to certain activities, thereby making him as unnatural as the famous 'economic man' of the classical economists. We see him only as an individual, forgetting that he is a member of a family, or only as part of a family group, forgetting his individuality: he may be noted only as a member of society, or only as a political unit, and we fit him into place in the mental map that we make of society. Here, we say, is a man; he is a father of a family, living at Nottingham, in the South-East Ward, and a parliamentary voter for the Southern Division. Thereupon we think we have him summed up; we treat him as a unit, and, mapping all England out into a number of constituencies and municipal areas, we plan out for him a new heaven and a new earth based upon his position as a political unit. We claim that he is now provided for in a democratic State, for he has the vote for parliamentary and local elections, and we have given the municipality powers to provide him with the decencies of existence.

But perhaps the man sees himself in a very different light and has quite a different map of England in his mind, where our constituencies and local governing areas fade into the background. Perhaps he is a keen churchman, and sees himself first and foremost as church-warden of St. Thomas's and the city for him is mapped out into parishes and the country into dioceses; or perhaps he is a keen member of the co-operative store, interested in a demarcation dispute with a neighbouring society, and his England shows a map marked by the conquests of co-operation; or again he is a keen Oddfellow or Forester, a past grand-master or chief-ranger, and all his interests are bound up in the welfare of his lodge or branch.

Again, he may be a member of the Notts and Derby Miners' Union, affiliated to the Miners' Federation of Great Britain, and his areas are the mining districts and subdistricts, and his annual conference takes the place in his mind of Parliament. It may be the man has none of these interests, yet he has something that marks him off from some of his fellows and unites him to others; he follows Tottenham Hotspur or Sheffield Wednesday at football, belongs to the Utility Rabbit-Breeding Society, or plays the big drum in the Silver Prize Band. To all of these your elaborate political divisions are secondary, and he does not see himself as you see him. Much of our trouble to-day comes from not seeing that England is mapped out into a very large number of conflicting and over-lapping circles, and from expecting that each man will be interested in the same set of activities and from trying to utilise only one kind of organisation.

Generally the social worker is too apt to consider only the religious, the municipal or the cash nexus of employer and employee, with the result that he tries to get things done through the wrong instrumentality. Industrial matters are best dealt with by organisations based on industry, matters affecting home life by those based on locality. There are some social reformers who look only to locality, urging the concentration of every form of social effort into the hands of local authorities. Some trade unionists, on the other hand, see the industrial side only, advocating the abolition of all groupings save that of industry, and substituting for our present forms of government a sort of glorified trade-union conference with subordinate trades councils. Others again can see nothing but the consumer, and would rebuild society on a basis of co-operative societies. All alike are short-sighted; men's whole lives are not concerned with industry, nor with locality, nor with religion, and different social machinery is needed for the satisfaction of separate needs.

Thus an examination of the great organisations, built up and controlled by working people for the better satisfaction of their wants, the friendly society, the trade union, the co-operative society and the club, will prevent us from over-simplifying the mechanism of society. Not only will they show us many examples of devotion and social service, but they will assist us to realise what are the things that working people themselves have found so necessary, that they have undertaken the work of providing them for themselves. Social workers are rather apt to think too much of what they think the poorer classes ought to want, and not enough of what are their actual demands. Further, at the present time the criticism of society as at present constituted comes mainly from organised labour. It is true it may be expressed by people from the middle-classes, and it takes an H. G. Wells to describe New Worlds for Old, but the success of such writers is greatly due to the fact that they give voice to what the many felt but cannot express.

FRIENDLY SOCIETIES

The earliest in point of time of the organisations that we are now considering is the Friendly Society, growing out of the Village Sick Club or Burial Society to the big National Society with its hundreds of thousands of members. The village sick club or burial society is of great antiquity, and is the parent not only of the friendly society, but also of the trade union, which is really an extension of the idea of mutual help from the domain of sickness or death to that of industry. To-day besides the great national societies there are numbers of smaller ones, and the movement comprises a very large proportion of the population.

What part, then, does the friendly society play in social service? First, it establishes a bond between individuals, and it may be noticed that the growth and extension of the friendly society movement from small isolated clubs to big societies with branches all over the country coincides with the break-up of the old ordered English society caused by the agrarian and industrial revolutions of the end of the eighteenth and beginning of the nineteenth centuries. The shifting of the population from the country to the town and from the south to the north, with the growth of great towns and large new urban districts, meant the breaking of many ties of mutual assistance. Many people talk glibly of the mobility of labour, and are inclined to be impatient with those who are unwilling to go away and find work in distant parts of the country, or to emigrate overseas, preferring to stay in congested areas where work is scarce or intermittent; but they forget how great is the wrench of migration to those on the border-line of poverty.

At home there is the shopkeeper who knows him and will give him credit ; there are friends who will come to the rescue with a whip-round when things are bad, and there is his intimacy with the customs and arrangements of the place to which he belongs. If he migrates all these ties are snapped, and if misfortune comes to him, he is among strange people and alien surroundings. Here is the value of the Friendly Society or the Trade Union : the member who migrates can enter a new circle with credentials which will gain him acceptance, and provide him with friends from the outset.

Thus the first importance of the Friendly Society is, as its name shows, the provision of friends, and the more alive the society is the better : hence the love of ritual which still clings to this movement as it does to some of the older trade unions and of course to the Freemasons : it serves to bind men together in the same way as family jokes and sayings bind together the members of a family, or common recollections and experiences draw together the old boys of schools and colleges.

But like other movements, religious or industrial, it suffers from the nominal member ; the keen members of the lodge who attend regularly and do the business are few ; the majority only send their contributions up and draw their benefits, neglecting to take advantage of the principles of common action and fellowship that can alone make the society a real success. Like the divvy hunter of the co-operative society and the nominal trade unionist to whom reference will be made later, they only join a society for what they can get out of it, instead of considering what they can do to help it. This applies perhaps more to the big societies than to the small local club where everyone knows everyone else.

The practical work of the Friendly Society in providing a form of insurance for its members against sudden expenses such as funerals or sickness is important, both as providing a way by which persons of very small means can save, and as being the only practical way for carrying out the administration of such a fund. The economical administration of benefits can only be managed by those who have a close knowledge of those who have claims on the funds, and, when it was found necessary to extend the provision of sickness benefit to the whole of the less wealthy section of the community by the National Health Insurance Act, it was to the co-operation of the experienced Friendly Society members that the framers of the Act turned to ensure that the funds should be wisely administered, and not be plundered by malingerers.

This Act may be regarded either as an interference with the individual and an intrusion of the State into matters best left to the persons concerned to provide for themselves, or as an example of the co-operation of the State and private associations of individuals.

It is not necessary here to go into the controversies aroused by this Act or to discuss its success or failure, but it is proper to call attention to the large volume of social work performed by the members of the Friendly Societies in its detailed administration, on committees or as office-bearers in the various societies. That large sums of money drawn from national resources should be handed over to associations consisting almost entirely of working men and women for disbursement to their members, even though under approved rules and close inspection, is a distinct step towards the recognition of the right of those most concerned to do their own business instead of relying on paid experts mostly drawn from another class to do it for them.

Friendly Societies vary considerably in type from the strict teetotalism of the Rechabites, with their consequently sound financial position, to some of a more convivial type; but the essential principles are the same, and that this form of association is not entirely confined to one class may be seen by reference to the many compassionate funds or benevolent societies carried on by some of the professions and businesses.

In addition to Friendly Societies proper there are organisations of a similar type of rather various social utility. The savings club, in which the members invest small sums, and from which they can obtain loans, forms a valuable counterpoise to the ubiquitous money-lender with his or her penny in the shilling per month or even per week. It must be remembered that one cause of the high rates of interest is the lack of security, and many working men and women have no security except their known character for honesty, which can only avail with those who know them; thus a very real want is supplied by these clubs to those who are suddenly called upon for what is for them a large sum of money. Membership of the club may mean the difference between ruin or a successful new start in life. Despite the large sums of money passing through the hands of the treasurers, examples of dishonesty are not common. I know of a club of this nature that makes very big advances to its members who are going hop-picking or fruit-gathering, but failure to pay up on return is extremely rare.

Less valuable are the various organisations such as slate clubs, where the money collected is shared out at certain intervals, sometimes for a beanfeast, sometimes for Christmas dinners or for holidays, often they are run in connection with public-houses, where whatever advantage may be gained through the exercise of thrift is apt to be set off by the amount spent for the good of the house in drinks. The friendly societies have been approved by all sections of social workers as tending to self-reliance and thrift, and some have lamented that the Insurance Act has taken away so large a part of the ground by substituting deductions from wages for the actual payment of pence, which is held to have an educational value, making the people realise that they are really paying for something themselves, so that they appreciate it more. Whether this is the real psychological effect of paying pence, and whether it has any particular value is a matter on which many people are somewhat sceptical.

TRADE UNIONS

Mention has already been made of the importance of the trade union as an experimental laboratory of political science. It is also the training ground of the working-class politician and administrator. It is commonly assumed that those who have not had the advantage of a public school education with a system of prefects have lost an invaluable training as citizens in that they have not learnt to command and to take responsibility. There is a measure of truth in this as a criticism of our system of elementary education, but it must be observed that valuable as the experience of a prefect may be as a preparation for the life of an army officer or an administrator of backward races, yet it does not give the experience that is needed to-day, that of governing in a democratic state. Men of what are or used to be known as the governing classes are prone to overlook the difference between the absolute rule over subjects, and government with the consent and co-operation of the governed. Army officers and colonial administrators are fond of railing against politicians, and denouncing the corruption and inefficiency of representative institutions, assuming all the time that the art of government is a very simple thing. It is: for those in a position to say to this man, "Go, and he goeth." The officer commanding a battalion is practically an absolute ruler, and the limitations on his power come rather from above than from below; he has not to undertake the far more difficult task of persuading others, who have equal power with himself, to take a certain view, or act in a particular way. Men who have been for some time in this position find it very hard to grasp the difficulties and essentials of democratic government, hence the almost invariable failure of brilliant proconsuls to make any mark in public life at home.

The trade unionist, on the other hand, serves an admirable apprenticeship for political life: even as an unpaid official in his branch he has to learn the art of working with men of his own rank—he learns responsibility as he progresses from branch or district to head office: he must learn to be self-reliant, to take responsibility and where necessary brave unpopularity. The leader of a big trade union to-day holds a position of very great responsibility and bears a heavy burden. It is no light thing for a man to recommend a strike which will certainly entail direct loss and suffering on the members of his society, on the other members of the community, and perhaps on the nation itself. It requires a strong man to tell the members by whose votes he holds his position that they are wrong, and that the action on which they are bent is not merely inexpedient but inequitable, yet it is only by making such decisions and exercising a right judgment on very complicated issues that the trade unionist can hope to reach the first rank.

The trade-union movement in this country has been honourably free from corruption : cases of misappropriation of funds are very few, and cases of officials being in the pay of the employers' associations (a thing not at all uncommon in some countries), or acting as spies for the Government, are practically unknown. The idea of a trade-union official as a sort of frothy agitator whose sole object in life is the fomenting of strikes, is one that dies very hard, and is still widely held in those circles of society in which knowledge of industrial affairs is almost non-existent. The average trade-union official has to work very hard for a not very easy employer ; for the trade unionist, if loyal, cannot be said to be a very easy master, on the contrary his demands are great ; and the salaries of officials are not excessive, while strikes mean heavy responsibility and not much kudos.

Of late years political responsibility has been shifting from the classes to the masses, and it is no small social service that the community owes to the trade-unicn movement that it has trained in responsibility the leaders of the workers, who are now claiming a greater share in the control of the policy and administration of the country. This service is emphasised at the present time by the many examples that can be seen on the continent of Europe of the advent to power of those whose ideals may be lofty but their practical experience of the business of government is very small. It is not merely those who appear prominently in public life who are thus trained by the trade unions, but the very many subordinates who take their part in the carrying on of the business of the country, the leaven of men who are accustomed to consider before they act and have acquired some experience of administration. Like the friendly society, the trade union forms a link between man and man, and latterly to an increasing degree between woman and woman, so that people, meeting together to discuss industrial affairs, are led also to formulate opinions on all kinds of matters of public importance. In modern society there is every need for the formation of group opinions, and for multiplying the means whereby those opinions shall be expressed and brought before the minds of those responsible for public policy.

A few years ago Acts of Parliament were passed with little reference to the opinions and ideas of those who would be most closely affected by them. Politicians or social workers from the richer classes thought more of what they considered good for the poor than of what the poor considered necessary or desirable. With the increase of legislation affecting the lives of the poorer citizens at every point has come a closer attention to working-class opinion. Organised workers to-day demand and secure that working men and women should be placed on commissions dealing with matters affecting their interests, and they take good care that evidence shall be given drawing attention to those facts that they want to see emphasised and expressing the policy they wish to see carried out. The trade union supplies an instrument whereby this opinion can be formulated and a supply of persons accustomed to putting forward cases. This has brought about a closer accord between the ideas of working people and the legislature, though this is, in part, due to the inclusion in the House of Commons of more working men. To take one instance: the idea of a standard rate of wages and a standard working day has been one of the bases of the activity of trade unions since they were first started, and has grown to be a definite part of the normal working-man's outlook on life, but up to recent times it had failed to obtain the acceptance of other sections of the community. To-day it is accepted not only nationally but internationally, and seems to be taking its place as an accepted principle of civilisation. It seems probable that in a few years the idea that an employer can work an employee for as many hours and at as low a wage as he pleases will seem as obsolete as the conception that it is right that one man should hold another as his personal property.

It is not necessary here to trace the growth of the trade union from the local or shop society with a few dozen members to the big organisation embracing the whole of a craft or industry, such as the Miners' Federation with its 600,000 members, or to detail the different types of union that compose the body of nearly six million workers in industrial association; nor is it germane to our purpose to describe the various phases through which the movement has passed or is passing; our business is to consider it as part of the machinery of society, and indeed to-day an essential part. Just as in the middle ages the industrial life of the community largely depended on the guild, so to-day it depends for its smooth working on the trade union. There are still to be found those who regard trade unions as pernicious institutions, existing for the fomenting of strikes and the restriction of output, carried on mainly in the interest of certain greedy officials whom they would describe as paid agitators. They do not realise that the inevitable frictions of the industrial machine would be infinitely greater if there were no trade unions and no paid officials, and that their immediate abolition would cause as much inconvenience as if we did away with the whole of the paid and unpaid judges and magistrates of this country and all the barristers and solicitors as well. Men do not quarrel because of the existence of the laws and the judicial system, these merely provide a convenient means of settling their disputes. There are a few people who are fond of litigation and there may be a few who are fond of strikes, but as a general rule both forms of strife are regarded as necessary evils.

The everyday work of the trade-union official is the composing of differences, and the amicable working out of the various agreements come to between masters and men under which to-day the greater part of industry is carried on. Given the present system of industry, and organisations of employers and employed are necessary for its efficient working. The Lancashire cotton industry supplies a good instance of this peaceable activity of industrial organisations; for the remuneration of the workers depends upon a number of factors affecting the application of lists of agreed standard prices. Here the application of the agreed rates to individual cases is negotiated by the representatives of the two parties with a minimum of friction. As the State has come to take a larger part in regulating the industrial arrangements of the nation, the trade unions have been utilised for the purpose of ensuring that the wishes of the legislature shall be carried out. It is one thing to pass laws and another thing to ensure that they will be put into operation; the series of Acts regulating industrial conditions deal with a mass of detail, air space, humidity, fencing machinery, methods of payment of wages, etc., and it would be quite impossible for a staff of officials, even if it were far larger than that of the factory inspectorate of the Home Office, to detect infringements without the active co-operation of those employed in the industry. The difficulties that beset the individual in making complaints are obvious, and it is only by collective action through the officials of their unions that the regulations can be enforced. The comparative failure of the early Factory Acts were due, to a great extent, to the lack of a sufficiently well-organised body to insist on their enforcement, and the fact that at that time the trade unions were not recognised—were in fact in the eyes of the law non-existent—made the work of the factory inspectors impossible.

Since those days legislative and administrative interference with the conditions of the wage contract have gone much further, and such an enactment as The Trade Boards Act not only recognises the existence of trade unions, but implicitly demands their formation as a condition precedent to its success. For the adequate representation of the operatives on a board composed of masters and men, empowered to fix minimum rates of wages for a whole industry, presupposes some form of organisation whereby these representatives can be chosen and the demands of the operatives find expression. Thus an ever greater share in the management of industry is being given to these organised bodies, and in matters affecting the industrial life of the people they practically form a State within the State, divided not by localities but by crafts and industries. The trade union, then, is now an accepted part of the mechanism of society, and from being a body mainly critical is becoming constructive, and herein lies its importance from the point of view of the student of social science.

Formerly the control of industry was considered the peculiar sphere of the employer; the workers were concerned with the defence of the individual against any lowering of the standard of life, or carried on offensive action for raising it higher, but took no responsibility for the organisation of the industry as a whole. They did indeed affect its organisation; where the trade union became so strong that conditions throughout the trade became standardised, so that all employers had to give the same terms, the effect was to cause a concentration of effort on the technique of the industry, the introduction of better machinery and perhaps concentration of control into fewer hands by the forcing out of business of the less well equipped or favourably situated employers: but this was hardly an effect consciously intended by the workers.

To-day the trade unions are claiming a share in the control of industry and are forced to consider the particular trade in which they are engaged as a whole and in relation to others at home and abroad. This result has come about partly through the increasing dislike of the workers to be regarded as hands, mere cogs in the machine, but more from the better economic education of the leaders, and a clearer apprehension of the industrial system. Workmen will not now accept the excuse that higher wages are more than the trade will bear without considering whether the trade is efficiently organised. Thus the gravamen of the attack of the Miners' Federation on the mineowners at the recent commission was not so much that large profits were being made out of which increased wages might have been paid, as that the business was being carried on in a wasteful way, and that the demand for a higher standard of life could not be satisfied without a radical change in the methods of extraction, distribution and utilisation of the coal. This tendency to claim control and accept responsibility for industry is comparatively new, but it has gained strength very rapidly from the fact that at every stage of the war the Government found itself obliged to take into consultation the leaders of the trade-union movement. Thus to-day the trade unionists, or at least those of them that think and lead the rest, are putting forward proposals that merit the attention of every student of social science, because the basis of their claim is that industry is to be regarded as a service.

In the industrial movement are many different currents of thought and feeling; much unrest is due to ephemeral causes, many claims that are put forward may be unreasonable and some of the claimants may be merely selfish, but underneath material aims there is a core of idealism.

In the trade-union movement are many men who never grasp abstract ideas, whose imaginations do not run beyond an extra sixpence an hour or an hour's less work. For example, at a recent big conference, when a resolution relating to taxation was being discussed, a delegate rose and bored the audience for some minutes on an obscure wage question in his own trade only remotely connected with the question at issue. The habit of sticking close to details of fact, while frequent in all classes, is very common among trade unionists, but the active minority, who do the thinking for the consenting majority, are to-day claiming that industry must be regarded as a social service. The same idea is found among some employers, as is shown in the very interesting proposals of the building trades' parliament wherein masters and men make the astonishing and novel proposal that the building trade shall be remodelled with the object of providing houses fit for people to live in and buildings worthy of a civilised community.

The vested interest of the members in an occupation, not as a means of making money, but as a service, wherein they desire to give good value to society, is akin to the ideas that do, to some extent, rule in the professions ; the doctor, for instance, is always considered as not only gaining his livelihood from his profession but as engaged in a war against disease, and as a rule a high standard of devotion is expected from the members of that calling. The organisation of a profession to-day is very much like that of a trade union, save that the employers are the general community ; indeed it has been said, somewhat unkindly, that all professions are a conspiracy against the public ; the lawyers, for instance, are in reality the most powerful trade union in the country, practising a form of syndicalism. The legal profession has been sufficiently astute to get its working rules accepted by the State, with the result that it is blackleg proof, having power to expel any member that fails to obey the rules of the society, and the general public accepts these rules, however illogical they may be, such as the rule that regulates the proportion between the fees of leader and junior. The tendency of all professions and businesses of recent years has been to become more and more closely controlled by the ruling body; thus the architects, dentists and surveyors endeavour to get their names confined to those who have qualified at their examinations.

Thus to-day the claim of every sort of worker to be dealt with through his representative body is increasing, and the demand of those in any occupation to control that business is gaining ground, so that we may expect that one of the problems to be solved in the near future is that of the relative position of the consumer and producer in the modern State, and the demarcation of their respective spheres of control.

Before leaving the subject of trade unions it is necessary to say something of women's organisations, which have received a great impetus through the large number of women that either permanently or temporarily have entered industry during the war. The women's trade-union movement offers considerable opportunities for social work for women of all classes. Trade unionism among men has been built up by years of experience and endeavour, and a tradition has been formed and handed down, so that there is no lack of experienced leaders to carry on the work; even where it is extended to new trades, experienced organisers can be imported from old-established societies. But among the great mass of women workers trade unionism is a new thing, and capable organisers are needed. The work of organising women has its own difficulties: the majority work in a trade for a short time only and then marry, others may work for a time, drop out, and rejoin, so that the continuity of service which leads to common ideas and common action, and the interest in the industry, because it is likely to be the scene of one's life's occupation, are lacking, and up till quite recently in most trades, and to-day in some, rates of wages were very low. It is notoriously hard to organise low paid workers, and there is plenty of work for those who feel drawn to it: for much good work has been done in the past by middle-class sympathisers. In the trade-union movement as a whole there is not much room for the outsider, though in former days the Christian socialists and positivists rendered much service by their advice at a critical time, and to-day there is still close co-operation between some groups of social investigators.

There is room, however, for those who are prepared to serve; but they must not expect to rule: trade unionists have shown themselves not unjustifiably suspicious of the outside sympathiser, and have failed to take advantage of his technical skill. The old idea that one man is as good as another for all sorts of work dies hard, and much trouble might have been saved by a more extended use of the draughtsman and the lawyer.

A particularly useful work that merits attention is that carried on by the International Association for Labour Legislation. Their aim has been to promote international agreement on certain matters of industrial law, such as the prohibition of the use of dangerous materials in certain trades, and generally to try to keep Governments in line with one another by bringing up the standard of the worst to that of the best. The importance of this work is likely to increase with the proposals of the Paris Conference for International Labour Laws, and, as the linguistic abilities of working-men are very limited, those who possess the necessary qualifications can assist in enabling the workers of one country to know what others are doing.

THE CO-OPERATIVE MOVEMENT

The next great working-class movement to be considered is Co-operation. Just as the trade union is an organisation of citizens in their capacity as producers or performers of services with the object of protecting their standard of life and ensuring a fair day's wage for a fair day's work, so the co-operative society is an organisation of consumers with the object of securing a fair article, fairly produced at a fair price.

There are, it is true, co-operative productive societies that are organisations of producers, but these form only a small part of the movement and will be dealt with later. The co-operative ideal is the provision of goods and services without the intervention of the middle-man. The doctrine of *caveat emptor* is all very well in small societies, where the goods and services exchanged are few and their character known to all; but in a highly complex society such as ours to-day, the buyer is very much at the mercy of the seller. Even in the early times we find constant complaints of adulteration of commodities, and of regrating and forestalling, the old terms for profiteering; if that was so in days when consumption was very largely limited to things produced close at hand under well-known conditions, it is very much more the case when the ingredients of a simple breakfast come from several different continents. Thus the co-operative movement is an attempt on the part of the consumer to avoid the consequences of his own necessary ignorance, and ensure that he shall get value for his wages.

To-day the movement may seem to us somewhat prosaic ; shopkeeping does not seem to us very romantic or idealistic, or a likely foundation for a new form of society, and it is difficult to realise that the thousands of large stores, the central depots, farms, factories, workshops and tea-gardens of the co-operative movement are the result of the dreams of an idealist.

It is not necessary here to deal in detail with the ideals of Robert Owen, or with the early attempts at co-operation ; nor shall we trace the history of the movement from the handful of Rochdale weavers, who, by their discovery of the device of dividend on purchases, found the way to keep their members bound to the interests of the store, and so laid the foundations of the commercial success of the movement, up to the big societies of the present day, with their forty or fifty thousand members, their imposing buildings, their bakeries, tailor's shops and coal depots. It is sufficient to note that the movement has spread all over the country, though more particularly in the industrial north and midlands, and that the societies are federated to form the wholesale societies that act as producing, distributing and banking agencies for the societies that are members of it. These wholesale societies do a trade of vast extent ; own ships, factories, and estates in England and overseas, and trade with the movements of other countries. The extent of the movement may be judged from the fact that there are more than three and a half million members, and that the sales of wholesale and retail societies for a single year amount to over £80,000,000. Our purpose is to consider its significance as a form of social activity.

First, let us note that it is essentially working class. It has been helped from time to time by such men as

Thomas Hughes, J. M. Ludlow, E. V. Neale and E. O. Greening, but the management of the business has been throughout in the hands of working-men. That such a business has been built up on sound lines with many successes and few failures shows how large a reservoir of business capacity there is in the workers of this country, and also how much of the spirit of social service. It is often argued that without the hope of big pecuniary rewards business would not be carried on, yet it is rare for the officials of the co-operative societies to leave the movement, despite the comparatively small salaries paid and the tempting offers made. The directors of departments of the C.W.S. are content with very modest remuneration compared to what would be given for similar work outside, because the movement is to them something more than a trading venture. Consider, too, the work of the pioneers of the movement, and the amount of, voluntary work put in by them in their evenings after they had already worked long hours at their occupations, and had little leisure to devote to anything outside the earning of their daily bread.

Secondly, the fundamental idea of the movement is that of making a trade into a service to the community rather than a source of profit to the individual. The point that it emphasises especially is that things of common interest should be under common control. The things in which the societies deal are mainly, though not entirely, the necessities of life; food, fuel, and clothing, and the movement is a protest against the idea that the necessities of life should be controlled by those whose only interest in them is to use them as a source of profit to themselves.

Thirdly, the co-operative store is the centre for

various other interests; it is true that many of its members are only interested in the dividend and not in the ideal side of the movement, but the co-operatives have never lost the early conception of the function of the society as an educative force. As a rule each society has its education committee and sometimes a library, and provision is made for the needs of the members on the intellectual and recreational sides. Lectures are given and classes arranged, and outings and co-operative holidays utilised to keep members in touch with one another, at which speeches recalling old struggles and emphasising the ideals of the movement will perhaps be delivered.

Fourthly, the co-operative store provides for an almost unconscious saving on the part of its members, the advantage of the store being not the sale of goods at very low prices, but a sale at normal prices, the profits being returned to the purchaser in proportion to the amount of his expenditure, and so considerable sums are available from time to time which can be used by the individual for exceptional expenditure or invested in the society. Thus an energetic society can find funds to use for the benefit of its members in extending the field of its operations, and there are places where almost the whole population is employed by the movement and where the whole town is owned by a society. Thus there emerges a new form of community organised on a basis of the needs of the consumer.

Here reference must be made to the early ideas of the movement, that of the union of producers co-operating to make the goods that they needed, owning their own capital in common, and working under self-governing conditions. Such societies still exist, but are not of very great importance except as an experiment, and the bulk of the productive work of the movement is done under the ordinary wage system, the consumer societies supplying the capital and exercising control.

The difficulties that the producing society has had to contend with are those of securing discipline, efficient management, and an adequate supply of capital, and it has not been easy for them to compete in the open market. The idea underlying the self-governing workshop has departed from the co-operative movement, but has reappeared in a different guise in trade unionism, taking first the form of syndicalism, and then that of guild socialism. The distinctive point of the new movement is that it does not propose to set up competing industrial units, but to organise industry throughout on a basis of control by the workers from the shop to the whole industry; its adherents also realise better the need for management. In one industry, however, co-operative production has had great success, and appears likely to establish its claim to be the most satisfactory form of organisation, and that is in agriculture. In Denmark and elsewhere on the Continent and in Ireland, and to a less extent in England, co-operative societies have developed on many different lines. Co-operative credit societies for the provision of working capital on easy terms to the members, such as the Raffeisen banks in Germany, stock insurance, small-holders' and farmers' associations have been organised, in order to eliminate the middleman and take advantage of the economies of collective purchase and sale on a large scale. Endeavours are now being made to reorganise agriculture on lines which, while taking advantage of business methods, will leave the individual producer the strong motive of interest in his own farm or holding, and Agricultural Organisation Societies in England and Ireland are conducting propaganda and organising to this end.

It is not always realised how inconsistent men are as producers and consumers—as producer, a man stands out for high wages and good conditions—as consumer, for cheap goods with little regard to the condition of their production. Hence the rather ridiculous spectacle can be seen occasionally of strikes called by trade union co-operative workers against their masters, the co-operative consumers, who are also trade unionists.

The co-operative movement, as has been indicated, is not confined to this country, and the relationship between the movements in different countries is of great interest, especially at a time like the present when world economic conditions are under discussion. The League of Nations is an attempt to bring the nations into political co-operation ; while international trade-union conferences do their part in looking to the general conditions of labour irrespective of the nationality of the workers, the international trading of the co-operative societies may be the foundation of an industrial League of Nations. Further, it at least provides a common interest, and brings about meetings between men and women of different nationalities. The ordinary prejudice against the foreigner is still very great, but will be best broken down by the realisation that so many problems are common to all nations.

Another feature that must be considered before leaving the co-operative movement is the importance of the woman member. Among working people as a rule the bulk of the expenditure, being on necessities, is made by the wife, and differences of prices and qualities affect her as manager of the household more than they do the man, hence it is natural that women should take an interest in the movement, and this interest has been much increased owing to the activity of the Co-operative Women's Guild. This association has not only taken a big part in influencing the policy of the movement, notably in the question of the conditions of employment of the co-operative employees, but has been the means on several occasions of voicing the opinions of the woman in the home, notably in the evidence given before the Divorce Commission.

THE WORKING-MAN'S CLUB

The associative instinct shows itself again in the Club, which is often sneered at as a mere drinking place, a less regulated public-house; but, although it cannot be denied that there is some ground for this criticism, yet the club performs a most useful function in society as a meeting-place for the exchange of ideas and for good-fellowship. Those who sneer at the club fail to realise what are the ordinary conditions of a working-man's home. They are usually people with plenty of room, with a dining room, study, drawing room and billiard room, and they do not understand what life is in a four-roomed or two-roomed house. The man after his day's work returns home to tea taken in the kitchen; there are elder children, perhaps with school work or other occupations, younger children to be bathed and put to bed, and the household work to be carried on. Where can the father go? He may have a parlour, but, if the family is large, some of the children sleep there, and, if it is not, he very likely cannot afford a second fire, while in poor districts he will not even have a parlour. Even the most domesticated require something else after the day's work than sitting over the fire and smoking amid the noise and discomforts of family life. The alternatives are the club or the public house.

In country districts the village inn is practically a club, though there is always the necessity of spending something for the benefit of the publican. In the towns very few of the public houses offer much to the more thoughtful man who wishes for quiet amusement and company. Our policy has been to make the public house a mere drinking place, give it a bad name and prevent the respectable from resorting there. Teetotal enthusiasts denounce it as the cause of all evil, with the result that, instead of the old kindly sociable inn or tavern, it has become just "the pub," the beer house, or the gin palace. It is true that of late years efforts have been made by The People's Refreshment House Association and latterly by the Liquor Control Board in their Carlisle experiment to reform the public house, and restore it to its old position, but these experiments only affect a small area, and over the greater part of England the public house is mainly concerned with selling as much liquor as possible in order to make a profit for the brewer. The public house should take its place as the natural meeting place for friends who wish to enjoy each others' society and a friendly glass. It may be that total abstinence is best, and that prohibition as adopted by the U.S.A. would be a wise step, but our present policy, whereby the whole interest of a public house is concentrated on the sale of intoxicants, seems to be absurd.

The rise of the club is due very largely to this decadence of the tavern. It might almost be considered to bear the same relationship to the public house as the co-operative store does to the multiple shop: in both is present the same idea of converting a profit-making business into a service controlled by and for a group of citizens.

We may divide working-men's clubs into three groups.

First, there is the club carried on by some organisation or individual by whom the funds are partly provided, where the control is not entirely in the hands of the members; these are generally run with some motive other than that of mere conviviality, for instance, to keep the members of some religious body together, to keep men or women out of the public houses, or as part of the educational work of a settlement. These are practically always teetotal and are not germane to the subject of this chapter.

Secondly, there is the club where the main idea is that of social intercourse and where all sorts of activities are carried on. Many working-men's clubs profess to provide instruction as well as recreation. Lectures are given on the premises, or there is a library, or a debating society, but the main object is recreation. Billiards and cards practically always, bands and choirs, football, bowls, or running or cycling may be provided. Here we have a natural and useful antidote to the public house.

Thirdly, the club may be one in name only, run really in the interest of a brewer who supplies the beer, from the sale of which the club derives its financial support.

The political club may fall into any of these categories.

There are many successful political clubs where no liquor is sold, and these are generally the most active in their political, literary, and educational pursuits. There are others that are mainly recreational, becoming galvanised into a sudden political activity only at election time, and there are some that are mere drinking places.

In the club of the best type all the members will be interested in its doings; it will form a real social centre, and the influence of its members may be great. In the more purely recreational types there will generally be a group of enthusiasts with higher ideals than the rest, who have to struggle to prevent the political or intellectual side from being swamped by the recreational or perhaps the convivial.

Those who wish to broaden the outlook of their fellow-men, who are enthusiastic for music, art or literature, will find here a good opportunity, for by joining as ordinary members, they can use their influence for furthering their ideals. It is important to remember that although everybody can, and most people do, read newspapers, public opinion is formed more by discussion and conversation than by reading, and that local affairs, particularly, are discussed in public houses and clubs, these informal discussions doing more for the circulation of ideas than public meetings and set debates.

An extension of the club movement to women seems to me particularly desirable. At present comparatively few women, particularly among the married, belong to clubs or societies, and those offered to them are too often of the goody-goody improving nature. If the premises of men's clubs could be utilised during the day, at such times as are most convenient to those concerned, for married women to come, with some co-operative arrangement for the care of the young children, it would be possible to widen the outlook, and stimulate a greater interest in political and social matters among those who, at present, are very little affected by other organisations. Married women have the vote, but very many are content to take their views from their husbands and, despite the risk of being charged with breaking up the harmony of the home, those who were foremost in the struggle to obtain the franchise would be doing social work of value by promoting such clubs, so that the vote may be utilised with some appreciation of its effect on the lives of this class of citizen.

WORKERS AND SELF-EDUCATION

One of the most interesting movements of the day is that concerned with the higher education of working people, and it affords an example of a movement essentially working class, originated by working-men, but one in which the middle-class man has been able to co-operate with the best results. There is an impression that education is something imposed from above by those who are educated on those who are not, by enthusiasts on the indifferent, and there is some truth in this view, but it ignores the demand for education that comes from working-men themselves. People are sometimes heard to say, " We are giving the people too much education," or " Reading, writing and arithmetic are sufficient for manual workers, why educate people above their stations in life ? " These views are old-fashioned to-day, and it must be realised that when once you have set the doors of education ajar you cannot close them.

The picture of the schoolboy going unwillingly to school is a half-truth. The average middle-class boy has little desire to learn, but a considerable number of working-men and boys are keen, some from a real appreciation of the value of education in itself, others because they see that knowledge is power. Economics is a subject not much dealt with in middle-class schools, and I have never heard of any great demand for its inclusion in the curriculum, but if you were to collect a number of working-men together, and were to ask what subject they would like to study, the majority would vote for economics or industrial history, because, as members of a class industrially subject to another, they feel the need of a weapon. This desire has been utilised by the Workers' Educational Association, which owes its foundation to a working-man, Albert Mansbridge, to promote education of a university type among the workers. Many classes are held in economic subjects by working-class organisations, particularly those that are political; a local labour party sometimes, a socialist branch almost invariably, will hold a class in the winter months for the instruction of its members: but without decrying the educational value of the work done in this way, it must be admitted that the classes are concerned with the subject from one point of view mainly: they are propagandist first and educational second.

The aim of the W.E.A. is to promote education as something of value in itself for the individual and the community: it is directly concerned with the endeavour to find out the truth, and will look at a subject from all points of view.

While most classes will begin with an economic subject, they will go on to literature, history or philosophy, for the aim of the Association is to supply a real university education.

As has been said above, the W.E.A. is the expression of the workers' demand for education, and this is its particular value, but this is not to belittle the work of other agencies in the past, such as the University Extension movement, the Working-men's College or the Polytechnics ; all these were expressions of social service on the part of those who originated them, and they met with a response from those who desired education, but they came from above ; the W.E.A. comes from below. Its essence is the democratic basis, and the relationship of teacher and pupils, which is that of co-operation in the search for knowledge rather than the teacher speaking *ex cathedrâ* to the students. The tutorial class, not the lecture, is its characteristic. The university man or woman who acts as teacher must get to know his class and be prepared to learn as well as teach.

The value of this movement cannot be overestimated ; the great danger of all democratic movements and of all extensions of the franchise is that power passes to the less educated. The generally anticipated rise to power in the near future of Labour would seem less like the end of all things to those who prophesy evil, if they could attend a tutorial class and see how the worker is fitting himself for his new responsibilities.

The W.E.A. represents more than this ; it is the claim of the wage earners for a full share in the achievements of the human intellect, and herein it provides an opportunity for university men who feel called to social service. The essence of social service is the desire to share with others advantages that they have not been able to attain, but in this case it is not even a case of giving money or anything material, but of sharing intellectual and moral gifts with others, with the certainty of increasing one's own store in the act of giving. For those who wish to take up public work there can be no better training than to join a W.E.A. class as tutor or member, and discuss the problems that arise with some of the best brains among the workers.

Besides the direct work of the W.E.A. it has a value as a centre for the formation of a working-class policy on educational matters. There are theorists and faddists of every sort in education, and it is well that those who form the bulk of the nation should themselves formulate their ideas as to the sort of education they require.

This need for education was also felt by the trade unions, with the result that Ruskin College, Oxford, was founded for the purpose of providing higher education to promising young men who were likely to become officials in their unions. Students are sent with scholarships provided from the union funds, and stay a year taking advantage of the traditions of learning attached to the spot, and at the same time influencing to some extent the other colleges. As a result of a dispute the Central Labour College was started in London, with the idea of teaching the pure milk of the word of class war economics, but they must be regarded as rather propagandist than educational.

A point very noticeable in the organisations of working-men that we have been considering is their inclusiveness. In Germany the trade unions are divided between the social democratic, the Hirsch Duncker, and the Christian sections, and in Belgium this division extended, at least before the war, to clubs, co-operative societies and even cafés, some being Socialist, some Liberal, and some Christian. Perhaps this gave more cohesion to the Belgian Labour movement than is obtained over here, but the nation lost owing to the segregation of the community on religious and political lines.

In England this difficulty has not appeared, and I think it would be disastrous if it did ; for at the present time, by the mingling of men of various creeds and opinions in common organisations, the edge of the differences is blunted and changes of opinion are not so much forced on a dissentient minority by the force of the majority as imperceptibly introduced, becoming familiar to their opponents before any changes brought about by their application are effected. It is one of the dangers of large societies that the members may get too far away from each other, and the meeting together of men and women from different parts of the country, who were little likely to come in contact in peace time, may be noted as one of the results of the war. During the war, whether by design or chance, drafts to a battalion seemed frequently drawn from the parts of the country most distant from that battalion's home ; thus to a battalion mainly composed of South Lancashire trade unionists was sent a number of lads from villages in Wiltshire, and their mingling in the close fellowship of the trenches is likely to have considerable effects on the mental outlook of both parties. Much the same has happened through the collecting of people in munition works, while the mingling of officers and men drawn from different classes should have valuable effects in creating better understanding between all sections of the community.

GLASGOW : PRINTED AT THE UNIVERSITY PRESS BY ROBERT MACLEHOSE AND CO. LTD

CPSIA information can be obtained at www.ICGtesting.com
231289LV00004B/53/P

9 781177 972468